The Divorce Helpbook for Teens

Are you looking for a Rebuilding seminar near you?
Do you lead Rebuilding seminars for others?
You'll find seminar information on-line at
www.rebuilding.org.
Dozens of locations in the U.S., Canada, and Europe.

RebuildingBooks™
Relationships – Divorce – and Beyond

The Divorce Helpbook for Teens

Cynthia MacGregor

Impact Publishers®
ATASCADERO, CALIFORNIA

ATTENTION ORGANIZATIONS AND CORPORATIONS:

This book is available at quantity discounts on bulk purchases for educational, business, or sales promotional use. For further information, please contact Impact Publishers, P.O. Box 6016, Atascadero, California 93423-6016. Phone 805-466-5917, e-mail: info@impactpublishers.com

Library of Congress Cataloging-in-Publication Data

MacGregor, Cynthia.
  The divorce helpbook for teens / Cynthia MacGregor.
    p. cm. — (Rebuilding books, for divorce and beyond)
  Includes index.
  ISBN 1-886230-57-9 (alk. paper)
    1. Children of divorced parents—Juvenile literature. 2. Divorce—Juvenile literature. I. Title. II. Series.

HQ777.5.M334 2004
306.89—dc22
                                        2004003707

Publisher's Note
This publication is designed to provide accurate and authoritative information in regard to the subject matter covered. It is sold with the understanding that the publisher is not engaged in rendering psychological, legal, or other professional services. If expert assistance or counseling is needed, the services of a competent professional should be sought.

Impact Publishers and colophon are registered trademarks of Impact Publishers, Inc.

Cover by K.A. White Design, San Luis Obispo, California
Printed in the United States of America on acid-free, recycled paper.

Published by ***Impact &*** ***Publishers, Inc.***
POST OFFICE BOX 6016
ATASCADERO, CALIFORNIA 93423-6016
www.impactpublishers.com

For Justin and Tori,
who've "been there, done that"

CONTENTS

Introduction 1

Chapter 1: It's Not About You — It Just Feels Like It Is 5

Chapter 2: How Did We Get Into This Mess? 15

Chapter 3: Your Comfort Zone 27

Chapter 4: A Life Full of Changes 41

Chapter 5: Parent Time: Custody & Visits 47

"What's New With You, Dad?" 61

Chapter 6: Parents at a Distance 71

Chapter 7: Unfair Tactics 77

Chapter 8: A Time of Turmoil 87

Chapter 9: The FAQ Chapter 95

Chapter 10: A Few Last Words 131

Index 133

Introduction

A few years ago I wrote a book called *The Divorce Helpbook for Kids*. Feedback about that book tells me that it has helped a lot of kids to deal with the issues that face them when their parents get divorced.

It's rare for a divorce to leave the kids of the family untouched. Even when the parents have been fighting horribly for a long time, and the divorce brings welcome peace at last, there are issues to deal with: absent parents who don't visit as often as they should (or as often as the kids might like); parents who use their kids to carry messages to the other parent; parents who use their kids as spies to find out what's going on in the other parent's household; and perhaps the kid missing the parent who no longer lives in the house.

Those are only a few of the situations kids have to deal with when their parents end a marriage.

The Divorce Helpbook for Kids was written for kids around the ages of eight to twelve. What about teenagers?

Being older, a teenager has a better understanding of what's going on. But teenagers have their own unique problems to deal with when their parents get divorced.

Fortunately, there's help for teens, too. You're reading it.

Some of the information you'll find here is different from what's in *The Divorce Helpbook for Kids.* You're older. There are things that are appropriate to say to you that wouldn't have fit in a book for younger kids. Some of the information is the same . . . but it's written for you. You're not in elementary school anymore.

But whether your parents are just talking about possibly ending their marriage, or are in the midst of a divorce, or have been divorced for a while already, I hope this book helps. I also hope I won't be the only one who's helping you. There are plenty of other resources you can call on if you're having a rough time with all that's going on in your parents' lives. Who or what are those resources?

• Your friends . . . particularly the ones who've already been through what you're now going through.

• A teacher you trust who gives good advice.

• A trained professional counselor. (This person might be called a psychologist, social worker, or family therapist, or perhaps by some other title, but he or she is specifically trained to help people who are undergoing difficult situations in life.)

• Your school counselor or psychologist, if your school has one.

• A clergyperson (minister, rabbi, priest . . .).

• A youth counselor or youth leader in a church or synagogue.

• An adult you're comfortable talking to, who you know gives good advice. This might be a relative, a neighbor, a friend of the family, or the parent of a friend.

• Other books, websites, and telephone helplines.

In addition, you may find it useful to keep a journal. Now, don't go rolling your eyes! I didn't say "diary" — I said "journal." Plenty of famous people — men and women — have kept journals. (Some have even kept diaries.) Your journal is your private property. You can write just the bare-bones facts, or you can include your emotions as well. What went wrong today? What went well today? What happened today that was different from the way things used to happen before your parents split up? Get it all down in the journal.

It will be even more helpful if you can include your feelings too: "I hate this garbage with having Mom and Dad in separate houses." "I wish Mom would stop yelling at me all the time just 'cause she's so unhappy. It makes me angry." "How come Todd can go live with Dad and I can't? It's not fair!" "I feel sad for Angie. She's taken this the hardest of all of us."

You can say things to your journal that you might not want to say to anyone else. And your journal is always there for you — even if you wake up at three in the morning and can't sleep. It's never busy with basketball practice or homework or any of the things that might sometimes keep your friends (or anyone else) from being available just when you need to talk to them.

Sometimes just writing (or talking) about the situation, what's going on, what you think about the situation and what you *feel* about the situation, is enough to help. Sometimes, too, talking or writing about the situation will give you a thought, an idea for the way to handle a particular aspect of the problem.

You can't change what's happened. You can't get your mom and dad back together. But you *can* change certain situations that may have resulted from the divorce. And you can learn ways to make it easier to live with other situations. (If a situation can't be changed, isn't it good if you can at least make it less painful or stressful for yourself?)

Keeping a journal can help you with all of this. Why not try it?

It's tough when you find yourself in a situation that leaves you needing help. But, if you are in that situation, I hope with all my heart that this book brings you some help and comfort.

Points to Remember

• It helps to tell someone what's happening in your life and what you're feeling.

• Keeping a journal can be helpful.

• You can't undo the divorce, but you can change some of the hassles that resulted from it.

1

It's Not About You — It Just Feels Like It Is!

The Algebra test you've studied for but still don't feel ready. Too many chores around the house! Teachers who give homework as if they think you have nothing else to do all evening but their assignment. Your little brother, who wants you to help him with his model plane and won't leave you alone about it. Boring family visits with adults you don't care about. Your best friend, who's in crisis over a wrecked romance. Stressing over the team tryouts on Friday.

Man! It isn't easy being a teenager, is it?

No, it isn't! And now your parents are getting divorced (or are already divorced), too? It isn't fair! Don't they have any consideration for your feelings? *Being a teenager can be a pain!*

Reality check: I know this breakup of your family is rough on you, but consider this: *Getting divorced is no fun for your parents, either.* They're not doing this *to you.* They're not doing this *because of you.* In fact, much as you may be hurting right now, it's important that you recognize that *the divorce is not about you!*

Most often, divorce is the pits — for everyone in the family. Believe it or not, your parents are hurting too — big time.

This book, however, *is* about you. So let's take a look at what you're probably going through right about now.

You're used to life kind of going along the way it always did. You're used to the (relative) calm of your home life. Yeah, sure . . . your mom sometimes yells at you to clean up your room. ("Sometimes"?! Okay, maybe she's on your case 24/7!) Sure, your dad is on your case too. He wants you to "Get an after-school job!" so you can contribute to your college fund, or "Quit your after-school job!" so you can study more and improve your grades, or "Clean out the garage!" (and a million other chores on a list, just waiting), or "Give up that #$&*$ garage band and spend more time *studying*" instead of blasting the neighborhood, or maybe it's all of the above.

But, way back in the "good old days," before your mom and dad started hassling you so much, life was a ton more peaceful. More calm. More bearable.

You know what? I bet your parents wouldn't be on your case so much if *their* lives were happier. I bet they'd leave you alone if they weren't so unhappy themselves.

What? Your parents unhappy? How bad can it be? They seem pretty much the same as ever.

I'll give you a hint. Parents don't always show their kids what's going on in their lives, their heads, or their hearts. Sure, you probably sensed that things haven't been just right recently, but now you know it's worse that you thought. And you're finding out that, when parents are fighting between themselves, they often take it out on their kids.

It's not fair! That's between them! Why are they taking it out on me?!

Because they're human. No, it's not fair. But now . . . be honest . . . are you always fair? Be truthful, now, haven't you ever snarled at your mom, snapped at your little sister, or even gone off on your best friend because you were having a bad day?

You're human, right?

So are your parents.

▼ ▼ ▼

When Andrea's parents' marriage started to go sour, nothing made Andrea's mom happy. And that included whatever Andrea did. Andrea's best friend, Lauren, had been through all this with her parents, who had gotten divorced the year before. "It's not you," Lauren told Andrea. "Try to keep out of their way till their marriage settles down . . . or breaks up."

"I don't want my parents breaking up!" Andrea answered. But that's just what happened. Andrea, a natural optimist, tried to look on the bright side. At least now her mom would be easier to live with. With Dad out of the house, Mom wouldn't be so unhappy. At least in that respect, life would be better now. But that wasn't the way it worked out. Andrea's mom was as unhappy as ever. She wore a long face constantly, never seemed to be happy, and was still displeased with much of what Andrea did. She seemed to yell at Andrea more often than ever now!

*Andrea didn't understand it, and neither did
Lauren. Andrea's mom had been unhappy in the
marriage, but now she was divorced. Why was she
still unhappy?*

▲ ▲ ▲

Divorce doesn't automatically solve the problems that
existed in a marriage. And sometimes it even creates new
problems.

People get divorced for many different reasons. Some
marriage problems no longer exist once a couple isn't
married anymore. But some problems can linger even after a
divorce. For example, suppose the husband is lazy, or
irresponsible, or both. This guy gets himself fired from job
after job, spends his time hanging with his friends, ignores
his family, sponges off his relatives. Even after that couple is
divorced, the ex-wife is going to have worries, because a
man like that is not likely to be very good about paying
child support, or helping with the kids, or doing anything
else to help the family he helped to create.

And that's just one example. Here's another:

Suppose the wife is mean to her husband, and he finally
leaves her. You'd think he'd be very happy to finally be out
of a marriage in which he's treated unkindly. And he
probably is. But suppose that money is really tight for him
now. He can barely afford to keep up the house payment,
the car payment, the food bills, and the other necessary
expenses. When he was married, he had plenty of money,
but now, for the first time, even with spousal support
payments from his ex-wife, he really doesn't have enough.
He's going to be upset and worried all the time.

There are plenty of other things that can bother people after a divorce and make them unhappy even though they're glad they got divorced. Let's take just one more example: Before the divorce, the parents home-schooled their kids. After the divorce, both parents must work to make ends meet financially. Suddenly the four-year-old is in daycare, the nine-year-old in public elementary, and the thirteen-year-old in public junior high school. If the local schools are educationally inferior, or have bad environments, or are unsafe, the whole family is going to be awfully unhappy.

There can be plenty of other reasons for a parent to be unhappy after a divorce. It isn't easy raising kids, even when two parents are together. Doing it single-handedly is even more difficult.

All the problems don't magically disappear when someone gets divorced. And usually there are new problems, too.

Because they're human, moms and dads can become short-tempered or impatient with their kids. They may yell a lot, or not listen to the kids, or demand unreasonable chores, or expect kids to act like they were grown-ups already, or. . . .

Parents may not even realize they're being unfairly harsh with their kids. Sometimes an older child — that means you, teenager! — needs to sit down with the parent and *calmly, not accusingly,* point out the unfair treatment, explain that the parent seems to get angry too easily, or to get angry out of proportion to the situation, or to expect too much of the kids, or whatever else may be causing problems in the parent's relationship with the kids.

As I said at the beginning of this chapter, it's not easy being a teenager to begin with. And it's not easy having your parents get divorced. Being a teenager whose parents are divorcing, or divorced, seems to double your problems and your stress, doesn't it?

One more thing I'd like you to think about before we end this chapter. Take a look at the sidebar below—Jeremy's story—and give some thought to whether depression may be troubling someone in your family. It's serious, and may require special help.

▼ ▼ ▼

Since Jeremy's dad moved out of the house, Jeremy's mom keeps to herself. She's quiet, withdrawn, subdued. She doesn't talk to him much. She doesn't even get on his case about cleaning his room. One night recently he got home over an hour after his curfew. He tiptoed in, hoping she was asleep already, but she was in the living room, listening to music in the dark, something she had begun doing since Jeremy's dad moved out.

She heard Jeremy come in and called out, "Good night, honey." Not a word about his being so late!

Though Jeremy was relieved at having gotten away with breaking his curfew, he sure didn't feel happy! Mixed with his relief was a sense of . . . well, the best thing he could describe it as was disappointment.

Not that he wanted his mom to get on his case! But . . . well, he guessed it was two things. First of all, even though he'd get ticked off when she would yell at him — in the old days — now it feels kind of like . . . like she doesn't care anymore. Doesn't care when he's late. Maybe even doesn't care about him at all.

And second, his mom just isn't herself in a lot of ways. This business of not caring if he comes in late, doesn't do his homework, leaves his room a mess . . . well, it's just a part of what has happened to her. And Jeremy doesn't like seeing her like this.

He loves his mom, and he can see that she isn't doing too well since Dad moved out. He doesn't have to be some kind of therapist to figure that much out. It's a no-brainer. But what can he do?

▲ ▲ ▲

Which is worse — to have one or both of your parents so angry at each other that they take it out on you . . . or to have them seem not to care what you do?

Isn't that question kind of like asking whether you'd rather be beaten up by a 400-pound Sumo wrestler or have a ton of bricks fall on top of you? The choice is rotten either way.

Is there anything familiar about Jeremy's story?

What Jeremy needs to understand — and you too, if your mom or dad is behaving like his mom — is that Jeremy's mom is depressed. Sometimes people react to unhappy situations by getting angry. (And sometimes they take it out on the wrong person — like the parent who's angry at his or her ex-spouse but takes it out on the kids, or on the people at work, or on just about everyone.)

Other times, people react by withdrawing into themselves. They seem to just shut down. They don't care much about anything. Not about what's for dinner tonight — even if it's their favorite. Not about good news or bad news, pleasures

or troubles. All they feel is pain. Unhappiness. Sadness —
maybe overwhelming sorrow. Or sometimes they don't feel
much of anything at all.

Sometimes, parents don't realize they're depressed. They
simply think they're "unhappy." And why shouldn't they be,
following the end of a marriage? (This is true regardless of
which parent asked for the divorce.) Some parents do realize
they're depressed but just don't want to talk about it. Or
they are concerned that, if they talk about their feelings to
their kids, they'll upset the kids even more.

Is there anything Jeremy, or any kid in his situation, could
do for his mom? One action that could help would be to
tell someone that she's having trouble. He could tell
someone he trusts that she seems to be depressed.

He shouldn't tell his dad. His mom and dad aren't a
couple anymore. But he could tell his grandma (his mother's
mother, not his father's mother), or his mother's best friend,
or even his mother's doctor. If his mom has a sister she's
pretty close to, Jeremy could tell her.

Depression is a pretty common reaction to divorce —
both for the parents and for the kids. (If Jeremy himself
were depressed, that wouldn't be surprising either.) Chances
are, his mom will overcome her depression with time. But
why wait? Why should she suffer? And what if she's one of
the small number of people who don't get over it soon on
their own?

There is lots of help for people who experience
depression, especially depression that is caused by something
specific happening, like a divorce or a death in the family.
Short-term therapy with a trained counselor (or even a

pastoral adviser — a clergyperson) can be very helpful. There are medications that can help, too.

It would be better for Jeremy's mom to get some help — either from medicine or from talking to a counselor or both — than to try to fight the depression on her own. It would be better for her, and it would be better for Jeremy. And if Jeremy starts feeling depressed, he should get help too. There's no reason to be embarrassed or uncomfortable about needing help. It's perfectly normal for people of any age to get thrown for a loop by such major life changes as a divorce.

Points to Remember

• Divorce is rough on everyone in the family — parents, too.

• They're not divorcing just to make you miserable. They're not divorcing because of you.

• If they're extra-rough on you now, it's because they're so unhappy themselves, even if they don't show it.

• The divorce may solve some problems in the marriage, but it won't solve all the problems immediately — and it might create new ones, too.

• If one of your parents is being very quiet, keeping to himself or herself, he or she may be depressed. This happens often after a divorce.

• It's common for the kids to get depressed too — but there are places where you can get help.

2

How Did We Get Into This Mess?

Sometimes a divorce isn't a total surprise to the kids. But more often it is. Let's look at a few scenarios:

▼ ▼ ▼

Jenny's parents sometimes got angry at each other. Lately it had been happening more often. But Jenny didn't think much about it. Oh, it certainly wasn't pleasant to hear her mom and dad going off on each other, whether it was a lot of little bickering that seemed to go on and on and on, or one of their periodic big blow-ups, which involved a lot of yelling and screaming. But as much as Jenny hated to hear it happening, she never thought it would lead to a divorce.

When her mom and dad were fighting with each other, Jenny would just go into her room, close the door, turn on her music — even louder than usual! — and block out the sound of the angry voices. After a while, the loud arguing would end, and things would be strained but quiet around the house.

This had been going on for several months when Jenny's mom sat her down and told her that the two of them, Jenny's mom and dad, were going to get a divorce.

Jenny was shocked. Of course, she knew that her parents had been fighting more than usual lately. But TV families had arguments and didn't wind up getting divorced. She had occasionally been at one friend's house or another when the friend's parents started bickering or squabbling. They always quickly took the fight out of the room, somewhere where Jenny couldn't hear it, but still it was plain to her that her friend's parents were fighting. So other people's parents fought without getting divorced. Why did her parents have to split up?

Naturally Jenny knew that some parents did get divorced, but it had always been someone else's parents. And that was precisely the point: This was something that happened to other people's parents — not hers!

———

Burt's case was a little different from Jenny's — his parents fought, and he knew it, but they'd fought all the time . . . ever since he could remember. They'd always fought . . . why were they getting a divorce now? They'd gone on fighting for years and years and years. And they'd stayed married. Why, then, were they going to get divorced now? Yet that's just what Burt's dad told him was going to happen.

Burt didn't understand it at all. If they'd managed to live together all these years despite fighting, why couldn't they keep on the way things had been? It just wasn't fair! He thought they shouldn't sneak up on a kid with news like this!

———————

Adam's parents were just the opposite of Burt's — it seemed they never fought. That's why it caught Adam totally by surprise when, one evening, they had a family meeting and explained, in an oh-so-civilized tone, that they could no longer live together and were about to get a divorce. A divorce? Why??! They never fought. They rarely disagreed. Why in the world would they want to get divorced?!

▲ ▲ ▲

Jenny's parents' experience is a pretty common scenario. There can be many reasons why parents suddenly start fighting more, although they never used to have more than an occasional argument. It's not important for you to know every one of these reasons, and your parents' specific reason is really just between them. They probably consider it a private matter. But to help you understand what might be going on, let's look at just a few of the reasons that parents sometimes start fighting more when they never used to, or why they get divorced even if they're not having lots of fights.

First of all, you need to understand that when people get into their middle years, they sometimes change. Their needs change, their wants change, and their feelings change. Of course, no matter what happens between your parents, they'll always both love you in their own ways. That's just a natural thing between parents and kids. Even if, right now, they sometimes seem more angry at you than usual, and so they may not show it very much, they'll still always love you. (And some of the times that they yell at you, they're probably not really angry at you. Chances are they're unhappy with the way their lives are going, or the fact that their marriage is falling apart, and some of this anger spills over onto you.) But, even though their love for you won't go away, other things change inside their heads.

One of those may be what they want out of life and out of their marriage. And their marriage together may be a casualty of these changes.

Some people get to midlife and realize that they haven't done all the things they wanted to do. They may feel they've not had all the happiness they wanted in life. Sometimes this really is because the marriage isn't satisfactory or happy for them. Sometimes it's for other reasons, but the marriage gets blamed.

The result may be an awful lot of fighting, or a divorce, or both. (Sometimes the person who's dissatisfied doesn't start fighting with his or her spouse — he or she just walks away.)

That may be what happened with Adam's parents — the couple who divorced so unexpectedly, although they never fought. There may not have even been any anger. They may have just been dissatisfied with their lives and with the marriage and, realizing that they weren't getting any younger, decided to end it and look for happiness elsewhere.

Another common problem that can lead to the breakup of a marriage is that the couple got married too early and/or too young. Maybe it was "love at first sight" — not a good foundation for a solid marriage. Not all couples get to know each other well before they marry, and when they do learn about each other over the years they're together, they may realize they were not right for each other, and grow apart.

Sometimes couples split up when one partner or the other falls in love with someone else. Usually that only happens if there are problems in the marriage already. Sometimes those "affairs" — as they are often called — don't break up the marriage; they end, and — perhaps with help from a marriage counselor — there is forgiveness and a new dedication to making the marriage successful again.

What happened with Burt's parents — the couple who had always argued to some extent, so that their sudden divorce took their son by surprise? There are a couple of likely possibilities. One is that they were doing a lot more arguing in private, but Burt just wasn't aware of it. The other is that they had been unhappy through all these years of conflict, but they stuck it out together until Burt was old enough that they felt more comfortable about breaking up the family. Some unhappily married parents stick together "for the sake of the kids" and divorce only when the kids are grown. They may wait till their children are completely grown and have moved out, or they may wait just till the kids are no longer very young. (Unfortunately staying together "for the sake of the kids" is often not the best thing for the kids.)

But regardless of the conditions in your family before the breakup, one thing that's very important for you to remember is that the divorce is not because of anything you did.

▼ ▼ ▼

Jamie's room looked like a typical teenager's room — that is, a mess. Her mother and father had frequent arguments with her about it, but to no use. Her grades weren't great, either, which was another thing her parents frequently got on her case about. She wasn't failing any classes, but her grades were a mix of Bs and Cs, with not a single A. Her father insisted she needed to study more. Jamie always answered that she did all her homework, she studied for all her tests, and she was doing the best she could.

"If you'd spend less time chatting and playing games on the computer and more time studying, we could be proud of you," her father told her. The words stung. Why wasn't he proud of her now? Jamie did study, wasn't failing any classes, didn't do drugs, did all her chores around the house, and hung out with a decent-enough group of kids.

Around the middle of her sophomore year, things got a whole lot worse between Jamie and her parents — her dad in particular. Nothing she did was satisfactory to him. Her music was too loud and was "garbage" to begin with. The condition of her room infuriated him. When Jamie got two more holes pierced in each of her ears, her father practically exploded. "It's not as if I got an eyebrow ring, or a bellybutton ring, or a bar through my nose!" Jamie protested. She thought wearing three little hoops in each ear was nothing compared to the piercings some of her friends had.

Nothing else about Jamie pleased her dad, from her clothes to her makeup to her interest in "New Age" ideas. Jamie's mother didn't approve of everything Jamie did either, but it was Jamie's father who was the real problem. They had frequent arguments, and even when he wasn't actively being disapproving, he never praised her or seemed to be pleased with anything about her.

Several times when he blew up at her, he hollered, "How is a man supposed to live in a household like this?!"

This went on throughout the second half of Jamie's sophomore year, through the summer, and on into the fall of Jamie's junior year of high school. Then her dad moved out.

Naturally Jamie felt as if he'd moved out because of her. They fought all the time, and nothing she did pleased him. Now he was gone, and at last there was peace and quiet in the house, but it came at a price — an overwhelming sense of guilt. Jamie felt that somehow she had driven her father out of the house.

▲ ▲ ▲

Jamie had done no such thing at all! Here's the story behind the story: Jamie's parents had become unhappy with each other and their marriage. Jamie's father was easily upset and angered because he was already dissatisfied with his home situation. Even if things were okay in his marriage, however, he still might have been unhappy with some things in his daughter's life. He would have disapproved of the condition of her room, the state of her grades, and much else. Disharmony between parents and their teenagers occurs in most families around these issues. But there's no question that he came down harder on Jamie because of his unhappiness in his marriage.

Is it fair? No. Is it right? No. Is it all too human and all too common? Unfortunately, yes.

When Jamie's father finally ended his marriage and moved out of the house, it's understandable that Jamie took the blame to herself. It's an understandable reaction in any case; it's even more so when the conflict between the parents isn't that obvious. In this scenario, it appears — wrongly — that the only person Jamie's dad was unhappy with was Jamie. When one of the parents breaks up the family and moves out, the kids often feel responsible.

If your mom and dad argued a lot (or gave each other the silent treatment) prior to their breakup, it's easier to understand the problem between them. But if they put up a false front and managed to keep up the appearance of a good marriage when you (or others) were around, the divorce is going to come as more of a shock. Not only that, but it would be harder to believe that things weren't right between them. Naturally you'd wonder just what the problem was. And perhaps, as Jamie did, you'd blame yourself.

There's friction between most teenagers and their parents, but it rarely causes either of the parents to move out of the house! The squabbling between Jamie and her parents and her father's displeasure with her certainly weren't the reasons her father moved out.

If *you* have any such thoughts about your parents' divorce, you need to get them out of your head. No matter how unhappy your mom or dad is or was with your lifestyle, your grades, the condition of your room, your choice of friends, or any other issue, *that was in no way the cause of their divorce or the reason for one parent moving out.*

Sometimes, too, although a kid realizes that the problem is between his parents and is not his fault, he can't help wondering if things would have been easier for his parents if he weren't around. For example, suppose the parents fight about money. The teenager may think, "If they hadn't had me, they'd have more money, and then they wouldn't be fighting." Or, "They disagree sometimes about how to discipline me and what to allow me to do. If they hadn't had me, they'd have less stuff to stress over, and maybe they'd still be together."

All parents disagree to some extent about child-raising. And many families have financial trouble. But in a solid marriage, the couple can disagree without it turning into a fight or an angry silence or a big problem. And in a solid marriage, a shortage of money — regardless of the cause — will not by itself result in a breakup. *So, it still isn't your fault.*

If your parents haven't been having loud and frequent arguments, you may wonder why they're getting divorced. And even if they do fight in front of you, you may wonder why this is happening now, when they used to get along so well. It's only natural to be curious about such a major disruption in your family's life.

Even though it's quite understandable for you to wonder, you need to give your parents some privacy and some space, and respect their rights. After all, you don't really want your mom tearing down your dad to you, or your dad dissing your mom by telling you all the reasons for the breakup and all the faults he finds with her.

And if one of your parents does start tearing down the other one to you, complaining about the way he treated her or the way she behaved that made him leave her, you might want to say, "Save that for your friends. He's my dad/She's my mom, and whatever went wrong between the two of you should stay between you two."

Just to make sure your complaining parent doesn't hear this as a defense of your other parent, or feel you're taking sides, you could add, "I love you both. I don't want to hear from either of you about what went wrong between you two. That's your business. I love you both, and I always will. So if you have a problem with Dad/Mom, please talk to your friends or your family about it, not to me. I'm still Dad's/Mom's kid as well as yours. Please let me be neutral."

Points to Remember

• Parents typically are at odds with their teenagers. That does not cause a parent to move out of the home.

• People who are unhappy in their lives — including people whose marriages have gone sour — often will dump their unhappiness on others. They will be more critical, more angry, and more easily triggered into anger, because they are already unhappy. The degree of anger they show will be out of proportion to the incident that they are reacting to.

• In a strong marriage, lack of money or disagreement over child-raising will not result in a divorce. In a weak marriage, even if there are no money troubles or disagreements over parenting, other issues might surface and cause problems.

• It is not your fault if one of your parents moves out of the house, no matter how unhappy with you he or she was before moving.

• Divorce can sometimes be a total surprise to the kids. Parents might fight for years and then suddenly get a divorce, or never seem to fight at all and then one day get a divorce. (And then, of course, there are parents who are fighting more lately, but the kids still don't think the problem is *that* serious, till the parents announce they're splitting up.)

• If your mom or dad *seems* more unhappy with you lately, it's very likely that it's because things aren't going well in your parents' marriage, so they're unhappy with *everything*.

• The reason your parents' marriage failed is their personal business — and you don't really want your mom and dad putting each other down to you anyhow.

3

Your Comfort Zone

▼ ▼ ▼

Since Bethany's parents told her they were going to get a divorce, nothing in her life seems right. It didn't even feel good when she was chosen to be head of the cheerleading squad. She'd worked so hard to become head cheerleader, and she'd wanted the position so badly. But now that she had it, it didn't mean so much to her.

Her emotions swung like a pendulum between sadness and anger, though she didn't share any of this with the kids at school, except for her two closest friends. She tried to put on a good front, though it was obvious to everyone that something was troubling Bethany. She wouldn't talk about it, though.

At home she wanted to talk about it, but her mother didn't want to, and her father, though he hadn't moved out yet, was hardly ever there anymore. He was sleeping in the guest room now, and he worked late almost every evening, eating dinner downtown, coming home only in time to go to bed. He barely said a word to Bethany's mom, and he wasn't around for enough time to talk to Bethany very much anymore either. Soon, he said, he'd be moving out completely.

The main thing Bethany wanted to say to him — and did, the few times she was able to talk to him — was "Why are you doing this to us?" She asked the same question of her mother, but her mom only got upset with her for asking.

It used to be that when something was bothering her, Bethany could go to her mom for comfort or advice. But now, here was the biggest, the worst thing to ever happen to her, and her mother was no help at all! She didn't want to talk about it and got impatient with Bethany for bringing it up. "We're not doing it to you," was all she'd say. "This is between Dad and me."

But it wasn't! It wasn't just between Mom and Dad at all. Couldn't they see what this divorce was doing to her? Couldn't they see that the whole family was torn up? Couldn't they see that everything was changing, nothing was the same as before?

Worst of all, perhaps, was this feeling she had inside. After thinking about it a lot, she finally put it into words: She had always felt the one thing she could count on was her family. That was the one thing that would never change, no matter what else in her world changed. And now that wasn't true anymore.

*Now even her family was falling apart. What could
she count on?!*

*Bethany didn't know whether it was her mom, her
dad, or both of them who wanted the divorce, but she
blamed both of them. It wasn't fair! They were ripping
the family apart! Everything was changing! She didn't
like it . . . and she couldn't talk to anyone about
it . . . and she didn't know what to do to make herself
feel better.*

▲ ▲ ▲

Most of us have something we do when we need to feel
more secure. Some people call a friend. Some people have a
favorite robe or sweater or other piece of clothing they put
on. Some retreat to a special place — a lake, a park, a tree,
a room, a chair. Some like to eat a bowl of hot oatmeal —
or cold ice cream. Many little kids have stuffed animals,
dolls, or other items that offer particular familiarity and
comfort.

If you're a girl and have a stuffed animal collection, at
your age you may just enjoy looking at the cute, furry
critters. I doubt that you spend much time cuddling the
bears or dogs, and even if you sometimes do hug them, I'm
sure there's a limit to the comfort you can get out of a
teddy bear at your age. (Although you might be surprised to
learn that the Red Cross gives out small teddy bears in
disaster shelters and they're very popular with adults, too, in
times of great stress.)

Fortunately there are ways a person your age can get
some comfort in the turbulent times surrounding and
following the divorce of their parents. So let's take a look,

now that you need comfort more than ever, at where you might be able to find it.

Probably not from your mom and dad. They may be too wrapped up in their own situation right now. Besides, you may be feeling just a little upset with them for getting divorced. If they hadn't gone and decided to get divorced, you wouldn't be in the confused, sad, angry state you find yourself. (As we discussed, they are hurting too, and they didn't get divorced in order to hurt you. At least one of them — if not both — felt the divorce was necessary. But *you're* still hurting and, whether it's logical or not, you may be a little upset with one or both of them.)

Pets can be a great source of comfort in tough times. Hug your dog or cat. Feel the furry love. You can even talk to your pet — you know you can say *anything* to him or her without fear that it will be repeated!

Even more important, talk to your friends. Some of them have surely been through what you're going through and can possibly give you advice. Whether or not your friends have advice for you, they can certainly listen sympathetically and let you pour out your feelings — sadness, anger, confusion, shock, and all the other emotional tornadoes spinning through you.

You can get comfort and/or advice from other sources, too. You can talk to close relatives, neighbors you have a friendship with, any of your friends' parents with whom you have a particularly trusting relationship, and of course professionals, such as a therapist, clergyperson, religious youth leader, or school counselor.

Don't be reluctant to tell your friends what's happening in your life. It's nothing to be ashamed of or embarrassed about. Remember, it's not in any way your fault that your parents are divorcing. And it's a very common happening. Plenty of families go through divorces. (Some estimates say that half of all marriages end in divorce — a sad statistic if it's true, but one that guarantees you have lots of company!) I'll bet you've got any number of friends whose parents are divorced — or, if they're remarried now, were divorced at one time. You're not strange or weird or different. (Neither are your parents.) So talk to your friends. Lean on them. That's what friends are for! Pour out your feelings to them . . . or ask them to do something happy with you, to take your mind off your family situation for a while and lift your mood out of the hole it's been buried in.

If you have a boyfriend or girlfriend, of course you can talk to him or her as you can with your friends. But if you don't have a boyfriend or girlfriend right now, this probably isn't the best time to start that kind of relationship. With all that you're going through, and your emotions in a jumble, it will be hard to evaluate how much of what you feel for this other person is real, and how much is really just need or gratitude or a "shelter" from the family storm.

When your emotions are ablaze, and your world is disappearing out from under you, it's easy to grab at what feels like a comfortable relationship with someone who seems to really care about you. But that's not the best basis for a solid relationship. And this isn't the best time to trust your own emotions. It's better to rely on your friends — or on a boyfriend or girlfriend you already have. (And *don't even think about* leaving home to set up housekeeping with your latest romance. That's a recipe for big-time failure and maybe even *another* divorce in your life!)

But there are other sources of comfort, too. What about your favorite music? It's more than a background noise, more than something to dance to, more than a collection of CDs or MP3s. It can connect with your emotions, soothe your frayed nerves, and be a great comfort to you.

Get lost in a favorite book. Not only is it good to read books like this one for specific help, but it's valuable to read books for pure enjoyment too. Whether you reread your favorite novel and get lost in its familiar pages and interesting plot, or read a book of humor and laugh hard, temporarily forgetting your problems, reading can be very good for you. (Tip: Digging in at school could help keep you occupied and focused on something besides your problems. And it couldn't hurt your grades, either!)

Anything familiar can be a comfort. Not only your favorite novel, but even your favorite videogame or other game, your favorite sport or activity . . . anything that will offer the comfort familiar things give us. It will remind you that, even though the foundation of your family has been shattered, not *everything* about your life has changed. You still have your favorite clothes, favorite books, favorite games, your friends . . . and, realistically, you still *have* both your parents — and their love — even though one of them no longer lives in your house.

Take comfort in your home, too. If you're remaining in the same house or apartment as before, find peace in your old familiar room. The family room may look different now: Did Dad move out and take his favorite recliner with him? The living room may look different: Perhaps Mom, wanting the feel of a fresh start, repainted the walls a different color or reupholstered the sofa. Unless you've moved, however, your room is still the same, a reminder that although some things change, other things remain the same.

And what if, as a result of the divorce, you are moving? What if Mom and you are moving to a smaller house or an apartment? What if you're relocating to another city? What if you're moving out with Dad? Then make sure you have some say in how your new room is fixed up. Make it a place of comfort for *you*, as much as you can.

There are limits to how many of your wishes can be accommodated of course. If you want to paint your room's walls deep blue or hot pink, your mom or dad might agree to it. If you want to buy a new bedspread and curtains, the question is whether the expense is possible within the family budget. If you simply want your furniture arranged differently, or you want to get some new posters to hang on the walls, that probably wouldn't be any problem. If you're sharing your room with a sister or brother, you'll have to take her or his wishes and tastes into consideration.

Above all, take comfort in the knowledge that you're still a family, whether or not you're living together. Mom and Dad are no longer a couple, but whether or not they're married to each other, they're still both your parents. And even if Dad or Mom moves to another city, and you don't get to see one of them very often, you're still family.

Even though your parents may no longer love each other, *they both still love you. And they always will.* (Actually it's also possible that they do still love each other but simply feel they can no longer live together peacefully and comfortably.)

Even if Mom moves out of town and you see her only a couple of times a year and have to settle for phone calls and email the rest of the time, she's still your mom. Even if, further into the future, Dad marries another woman, he's still your dad. Even if this other woman has kids, and Dad inherits a whole new family by remarrying, he's still your dad.

He'll always be your dad. And your mom will always be your mom. And they'll always both love you.

They'll love you because they're your parents, and parents just naturally love their kids. And they'll love you because — as we discussed in chapter 2, but it bears repeating — the divorce was in no way your fault . . . no matter how upset with you your parents may have seemed to be around the time of the breakup.

Both your parents are still your parents. And your sisters and/or brothers are still your sisters and brothers, whether you're all living together or whether your sister is living with your mom while you live with your dad now. No matter who lives where, they're still your sisters and brothers (even if there are times when your brother is a pain in the butt and you wish you weren't related).

Meanwhile, here you are with this mix of emotions — probably mostly anger and/or sadness — wondering what to do about them.

Here are some ways to get anger out of your system for a little while: Hit a pillow — punch it as hard as you can with your fist or smack it sharply with a tennis racket. Throw a basketball hard. Bounce it on the ground or aim for the backboard — never mind the basket — and throw with all your strength. Hit a softball. Take your ball and bat to an open field or vacant lot, a softball field that's not in use, or any other suitable location, throw the ball up in the air, and swing with all your might. Or enlist a sympathetic friend to pitch to you. (Run after the ball yourself after you hit it. And really *run*. Pound the dirt as you chase after the ball. Stomp the ground hard, and run fast.) Do gymnastics, or any kind of vigorous exercise. Run around the block. If you have a private place where no one will hear you — maybe even at home when no one else is there — yell. Yell as loud as you can. And if you can't yell, sing at the top of your lungs. (Don't do anything that would lead the neighbors to think you're in trouble, though. You don't want to invite a visit from the local police to find out who's beating you!)

Exercise of almost any kind can be helpful. Getting exercise is a healthy thing to do for yourself to begin with, but in this case, it also helps get some of the anger out temporarily. Walk, run, shoot hoops, swim, ride a bike — whatever form of exercise you enjoy. (This is not the time for extreme sports, though. In your present state of mind, you might be tempted to take unsafe chances with daredevil skateboarding or other potentially dangerous activities.)

The actions I've suggested are all good for *temporary* release of anger energy. If you're carrying around a lot of anger for more than a couple of weeks, however, have a chat with your school counselor or clergyperson about it. (But don't let anybody tell you it's *sin!* Anger is very normal, very human.) Long-term anger isn't healthy, and you need help to deal with it properly.

And if you're feeling more sadness than anger? Cry — it doesn't mean you're a baby. Cry whether you're a girl or a guy. If you can't just let the tears flow unaided, rent a movie with a good sobby ending. Or watch a happy movie, or better yet a funny one, to cheer your mood, even if it helps for only a little while. Another way to deal with your sadness: Write about it in that journal I suggested in the introduction to this book. Or, if you're the creative sort, write a story about a kid whose parents have gotten divorced, or a poem about your feelings, or even a play.

▼ ▼ ▼

Danny's parents recently told him they were getting a divorce. He wasn't totally shocked; they'd been fighting pretty badly for the last few months, and he'd wondered how they could stay married, how they could still love each other, and fight the way they were.

He talked to his dad about the divorce. "I won't get into the reasons behind the divorce," Danny's dad said. "That's between your mom and me. Let's just say we can't live together anymore, and let's let it go at that. But you can ask me anything else you want, or just talk to me. Spill your guts. You'll feel better."

Danny did talk to his dad, but he found that he got more out of talking to his friends. His best friend's parents were still married, but another kid, Zac, who he was pretty good friends with, had gone through his parent getting divorced about a year and a half earlier. When Danny told Zac about how he felt, and how angry he was at his parents for breaking up, Zac understood what Danny was talking about, what he was feeling, and why. And he had some pretty good advice for him, as well as the answers to a lot of Danny's questions.

Soon Danny started spending more time with Zac than with any other friend. And he was always going to Zac's house, rather than having Zac over at his house. Zac understood. "Home's not a very easy place to be right now, is it?" he asked. Danny even slept over at Zac's house once or twice a week.

Danny wasn't a very athletic kid, but Zac got Danny to do some football drills with him. Pounding up and down the empty field near Zac's house, fighting each other for possession of the ball, helped Danny work some of the anger out of his system. Zac was on the school wrestling team, and he showed Danny some wrestling moves. The two boys wrestled on mats in Zac's basement, and the physical exertion was good for Danny, too.

One day Zac called and told Danny to meet him at his uncle's house on Elm Street. Danny knew the place Zac meant; there was an old shed there that Zac's uncle was planning to tear down. When he got there, he found Zac had brought a box of nails and a hammer. "What are you going to do?" Danny asked, thoroughly confused.

"I'm not gonna do anything — you're gonna pound these nails into this wall," Zac said.

"Why?" Danny asked. "Isn't your uncle going to knock this down anyway?"

"Just do it," Zac said.

Danny picked up a nail, pounded it lightly to get the point into the wood, then lightly tapped the nailhead with the hammer.

"No. Hit it hard. As hard as you can!" Zac told him.

"What's this all about?" Danny asked suspiciously.

"Just do it," Zac said again.

So Danny hauled back and whammed the nail with the hammer with all his strength.

"Good. Again!" Zac said.

Danny whammed away at the nail . . . again and again and again.

"Do it! Hit that nail! Hit it!" Zac yelled.

Danny really slammed the nails . . . he was working on his fourth one by now. Bang! Bang! Bang! Bang!

After about ten nails, Danny's body began to sag. He was tired, but it was a good tiredness. Sometimes lately, since his parents had told him they were divorcing, Danny had felt like nothing mattered anymore. He just didn't care — about anything. And he felt overwhelmingly tired. But this was a different kind of tiredness — a good tiredness, a healthy tiredness.

"Okay, let's go," Zac said.

"Where now?"

"Central Cinema. There's this really stupid comedy playing. It's just what you need."

"Nothing feels funny these days."

"Did hammering the nails make you feel better?" Zac asked.

"Yes," Danny said. "How did you know?"

"My dad got me hammering nails one day when I was mad about something. I felt better afterward. I figured it would work for you too. And you know how Coach Morgan is always carrying on about the benefits of exercise. This may not be what he had in *mind . . . but it works, okay? So trust me . . . and let's go to the movies."*

Zac was right. For now, Danny had worked some of the anger out of his system by hammering the nails, and he was in a better condition to laugh at something . . . and the movie really was stupid, and funny. For as long as he sat in the theater, Danny laughed at the movie and forgot about his problems.

When they came out of the theatre, Danny remembered his problems all over again, but at least he'd had a break from thinking about them. He'd laughed a lot during the movie. And he still didn't feel so angry — the hammering had certainly helped. He went home feeling better than he had in a long time. And he decided he was going to talk to the coach tomorrow about his angry feelings.

▲ ▲ ▲

Points to Remember

• Before the divorce, you probably felt comfortable at home and felt you could talk to your parents when something was bothering you. Now home is where the problem is, and your parents are the problem. So it's tough to know where to go to find the comfort you need

• There are many people who can be a source of comfort and advice now.

• There's no reason to be ashamed or embarrassed about the family's situation. Divorce happens in lots of families, and the fact that your parents are divorced is certainly not your fault!

• Now is not the best time to start a new romantic relationship.

• There are other sources of comfort, too: music, books, pets, hobbies, favorite places. . . .

• Old familiar things can bring comfort, too.

• You still *have* both your parents and their love, even if one of them will no longer be living with you.

• Exercise is a good way to get some of the angry feelings out and feel better for a while, but if your anger stays with you for more than a week or two, talk to a counselor or other adult you trust for some help in dealing with it.

4

A Life Full of Changes

As if it weren't tough enough that one of your parents is no longer living in your house, your life is likely to spring other changes on you now, too.

What are some of them?

• You — or the divorce court — may decide that you will live with one parent or the other. Or you may divide your time with both.

• If your mom (or dad) didn't work before this, she (or he) is likely to start working now.

• If both your parents were already working, one of them may need to change jobs, take a full-time job instead of a part-time job, work longer hours at an already-full-time job, or even take a second job to help make ends meet financially.

• Money is likely to be tighter. This may mean fewer luxuries, such as going to the movies, dinners out, or clothes you don't really absolutely need. (You may find them saying, "We can't afford those expensive sport shoes anymore. You'll have to settle for a less-expensive brand.")

• You may be asked to do more chores around the house, now that there's only one parent in the home. If your dad's moved out, for instance, Mom's got to do almost everything herself unless she can assign a chore to you (or to your sisters and brothers, if you're not an only child). You may find yourself asked to mow or rake, or fix things around the house, or do laundry, dishes, or some of the cooking.

• If Mom's gone back to work after being a stay-at-home mom and head chef previously, you may find that dinners are simpler and plainer since she has less time to cook — or dinner may be take-out or delivery more often than before. (I know you won't complain about pizza or wings, but eventually you'll miss having Mom's lasagna or roast chicken or other special dinners as often as you're used to.)

• If you have a younger brother or sister, it might be necessary to hire someone to take care of him or her during the work day. This may mean that Jimmy or Alicia doesn't stay home during the day anymore, or that Mrs. Miller comes to the house to take care of Jimmy or Alicia while the rest of you are at work or school. Maybe she's still there when you get home from school.

• You may have to move to a smaller, more affordable house or even to an apartment. The cost of rent on an apartment usually is less expensive than a mortgage payment on a house. Also, in an apartment building you may have a building superintendent who can change ceiling light bulbs and repair dripping faucets, and you never need to worry about who's going to mow the lawn. (Unhappy at losing your big backyard and the basketball backboard on the garage? Maybe the trade-off is not all bad. You can be grateful that these chores aren't falling on your shoulders!)

• Sometimes divorce papers call for the family home to be sold and the money split between Mom and Dad. In that case, too, you'd be moving to an apartment, to a different house (probably a smaller one), or perhaps even to another relative's house. (It might be fun for you to go live with Grandma or Aunt Brenda for a while!)

• You may have to adjust to going to a new school, making new friends, and everything else involved in moving to a new neighborhood or even a new town. (Life's rough sometimes, isn't it?!)

• You may find yourself moving with your mom or dad to a different area altogether. Now that they're on their own, Dad may want to live closer to work (which might be in a nearby city and not in the community where you live), Mom may want to be closer to her own mom, or they may choose cities with better-paying jobs

• Of course the biggest change of all is not having one of your parents living with you anymore. It's going to feel weird *visiting* your *dad or mom*! Parents aren't people you visit — parents live in your house! Well, not anymore.

Visiting your dad or mom on Saturdays or Sundays, or every other weekend, or for several months of the year — whatever the arrangement is — will mean at least a couple of things have to change in your life. First of all, one of your parents isn't there all the time — when you want to ask for advice. Or maybe you need help with history homework and the parent who excelled in English and French can't remember what year the War of 1812 was fought. Or maybe it's just a special time when you want to talk to the parent who's not around anymore. Of course, you can call on the phone, or email — but that's not really as good.

If you're used to hanging out with your friends on weekends, you might find yourself saying, "Sorry, but I'll be at my dad's on Sunday," or "Sorry, but I'll be at my mom's this weekend." (Although you might be able to have your friends visit you at your dad's or mom's house, depending on how far away you've moved.)

• Your dad or mom might even move out of town. I don't mean just to the nearby city or the suburbs, or, if you live in the suburbs, another suburb nearby. I mean really out of town. Like, if you live in Chicago, Dad might move to Seattle. If you live in Phoenix, Mom might move to Atlanta. You get the idea. Your dad might become an "out-of-town dad," a dad you see only on long school holidays like Christmas break, spring break, and summer vacation.

Some parents try to keep their moves and other changes to a minimum, but as we've discussed, life is not always fair! When your parents divorce, lots of things in your life change!

Points to Remember

• Divorce usually results in many other changes in your life besides the breakup of your parents' marriage.

• One of these changes is likely to be that the parent you're living with has less money than before.

• Obviously, one of your parents won't be living in the same house with you anymore. And though he or she is most likely to live nearby, he or she might have to move out of town, perhaps far away.

• You may have to move and change schools, make new friends, find new activities, and make other adjustments.

5

Parent Time: Custody and Visits

Maybe your parents have just announced their intention to get divorced. Or maybe they're living separately already but haven't been through a divorce hearing yet. Or maybe they're divorced already. If they are divorced already, you know which parent you're going to be living with. Just in case you don't know yet for sure, however, let's talk about that a little bit before we move on to talking about time you'll spend with your other parent.

"Custody" is a pretty complex legal idea that divorce courts use to decide how parents will divide up the job of caring for the children after a divorce. There are different ways custody can be ordered by the court, but most plans call for you to spend some time with each of your parents. Probably the most common arrangement is for you to live most of the time with one parent — that's known as "primary custody" — and for you to live with the other parent for short periods at various times — that was commonly known as "visitation," although the term isn't used much anymore. "Joint custody" is common now.

If your parents both live near your school, you might live with each of them about half the time. Or you may be at Mom's house during the week, and at Dad's on the weekends. A common arrangement is two weekends a month, one additional Saturday (or Sunday), and every Wednesday for several hours after school. Some families agree to place the kids with Mom during the school year and with Dad for holidays and summer vacation. Many other arrangements are possible too. There are lots of ways to set up a parenting plan. It's important that you tell your parents and the judge what *you* would like while the decisions are being made.

Although many parents — and most kids — would like to work out some kind of "equal time" schedule, in real life it's usually not possible to divide your time down the middle. Some negotiations will take place around setting up a schedule that works for everybody — taking into account your parents' work schedules, how far apart they live, your school schedule, your after-school activities, and other factors. It may not seem so at the time, but the court is required to take *your best interests* into account in making these decisions. Everyone will have to compromise some to make this work, so don't hesitate to make your wishes known, but be cool with whatever the judge finally orders. Even if the deed is done and it's not exactly what you wanted, you can make it work, and grousing about it won't change anything.

Where Will You Live?
Most often the kids live with the mother, but sometimes the dad provides the primary home for one or all of the kids in the family.

- The judge might decide that the girls will live with the mother and the boys with the father.

- If the dad works out of a home office, and the mom works away from the house, the parents might agree — or the judge might decide — that it's better for the dad to have primary custody.

- If Mom is going to school at night and working during the day, or plans to do so, it might be decided that the kids should live mostly with Dad — at least until Mom is through with school and can spend more time at home.

- Dad might want to have primary custody of the kids, and Mom might agree for any of a number of reasons.

- Sometimes the judge will listen to the wishes of a child old enough for his or her opinion to be considered. If you're in high school, maybe even junior high school, there's a chance the judge will take your wishes into consideration, especially if you can give a particular reason that you'd rather live with one parent or another. (In California, for example, judges are required to give serious consideration — the courts call it "due weight" — to the child's preferences.)

Talk to the parent you prefer to live with. Ask him or her if that's agreeable. If you're a girl, your dad may feel you'd be better off with your mother because she can better help you with some of the issues that arise as a girl grows up; the same is true in reverse for a mom and her son. Or the parent you'd prefer to live with may plan on working a second job now and not being home very much, or may already have picked out a new place to live that has only one bedroom. There are plenty of reasons why a parent who loves you very much might still feel it's not a good plan to have you live with her or him.

If both parents agree to have you live with the parent of your choice, the judge is quite likely to agree to the plan. If your parents don't agree, you can ask to be present at the divorce hearing, or to meet privately with the judge, so you can present your reasons for wanting to live with your dad or your mom. Have a list ready, and be prepared to try to persuade the judge. Try to come up with better reasons than "Mom's too strict" or "I love Dad better" or "Mom's house is closer to school/my best friend/the mall" or "Dad won't let me watch my favorite TV shows." (But do be honest; don't make up reasons.) Are any of these true for you?

• Mom gets angry and slaps me sometimes. Dad never does.

• My religious beliefs are more like Mom's than Dad's.

• Mom expects me to act like an adult when Dad isn't home. But I'm still just a kid. I feel pressured to grow up.

• If I live with Dad, I'll have to get a job because he can't afford to pay for my trumpet lessons and swim team fees.

• Mom works all the time and can't ever take me to soccer practice or make it to my games.

Your parents and the judge may agree on a joint custody arrangement in which you live with each of the parents for half a week, or for one week at a time. (This works better when both parents live in the same school district, but it's not impossible when they don't.) As mentioned above, this hardly ever turns out to be an "equal" division of your time.

Whichever parent you wind up living with after the divorce, you'll probably still get to see the other one fairly often, unless your mom and dad wind up living in cities that are very distant from each other. (Fortunately, that doesn't happen all that often, but it does happen. There are reasons why one parent or the other might feel it's necessary to move far away. We'll get to that in the next chapter.)

Visiting With the Other Parent

Whichever parent you don't live with will have the right to see you on certain days. If your parents get along reasonably well after the divorce, can talk to each other without fighting, and are fairly cooperative, they can arrange between themselves for you to visit at times other than what the divorce decree calls for. Maybe your dad wants to see you an extra evening, or an extra weekend day. Maybe the weekend you're scheduled to see your dad is the weekend of your grandmother's birthday (your grand-mother on your mom's side). Or maybe the weekend you're supposed to stay home with your mom, your uncle (on your dad's side) is going to be in town visiting from Canada. If your parents communicate well, they can agree between them to change the visiting days around.

It's going to feel weird going to *visit* your dad (or mom)! You may even find that talking to him is kind of awkward and strained. This happens for several reasons. First of all, the whole situation is weird and awkward — going to visit your dad, who should be living in your house, and seeing him in strange surroundings too. This can put you off and leave you feeling out of place and awkward.

What Will You Talk About?

The idea of talking to your dad at certain times is strange. You were used to having him home (at least much of the time, when he wasn't working, or bowling, or out with his friends). You were used to having him there to talk to when you felt like it, and you weren't expected to talk to him when there was nothing to say or you didn't feel like talking.

Now you are together for four hours or two days, and you're expected to sit down and have a conversation. Now is the time to catch each other up on what's been going on in your lives, make up for all the time that you and Dad weren't under the same roof, and cram the news of the past few days or weeks into one awkward conversation.

Plenty of kids in that position find themselves thinking they have nothing to talk about.

If you're a girl, your visits with Dad can be even more awkward. Some of the things that happen in your life just aren't things you'd be comfortable discussing with your father. Likewise, there are things that some guys don't want to talk to their moms about. Add in the things you don't think they'd be interested in, and it cuts down the possibilities for conversation.

Although at first it may seem that you don't have much to talk about with the parent you don't live with most of the time, don't give up easily! Keep in mind that you're a young adult now, and issues of the day that are of concern to adults will be affecting you soon, even if they don't already.

Here are just a few suggestions that may help you get conversations going when things get too quiet or boring:

• **Books/Movies/TV:** Have you recently read a book or magazine article that was particularly interesting? How about a favorite movie or TV program? Do you think your parents should still monitor and "censor" movies you go to, or programs you watch on TV?

• **Music:** If there is anything that usually separates the generations, it's music, but can you have a conversation with your Dad or Mom about your faves? Maybe you can explain what you like, not with the idea of "converting" him or her, but just as a way of telling them who you are. And don't overlook the possibility that you might find something to like about their choices too!

• **Money:** If you don't have your own bank account, or if you've never balanced a checkbook, or if you don't know about the power of compound interest, those are topics you really should bring up with both parents, so you can learn all you can before you're out on your own. Credit cards, for instance, can be dangerous in the hands of an inexperienced teen!

• **College and Career:** Have you made a decision about college — where you want to go and what you want to study? Have you talked it over with your mom and dad to get their ideas and support? Will you have a job while you're in school? Do you really know what it will cost to attend? How about preparing yourself for job interviews? Could your folks help you make some contacts to improve your chances of getting hired? And what about their careers?

Wouldn't it be interesting to find out what Mom and/or Dad really do at work all day (or night)?

• **Cars:** If you don't have your own car yet, it's probably only a matter of time. Do you know anything about how to select a car? How to take care of it once you own it? The cost of insurance, maintenance, financing, license taxes? Your folks have been there, and they could be of help, if you'll open up the subject.

• **Political issues:** Is there a big election coming up? Is the local Parks and Recreation Board considering programs for teens? Has the budget for schools been cut, so classes are larger? Is the national government considering a mandatory public service or military enlistment for young adults? Have you had a political disagreement with a teacher?

• **Philosophy/Religion/Ethics:** Are students at your school debating right-to-life vs. abortion rights? Is the pledge of allegiance a big issue in your town? How do you feel about prayer in school? Do some of your classmates pressure you to help them cheat on tests?

And there are dozens of other topics: loving relationships (including sex), getting along with siblings or cousins, chores and home maintenance (you'll have your own home one day!), cooking (will you be ready to prepare your own meals when you leave home?), hobbies, health, pets . . . the list goes on. You may be surprised at how much fun it can be, and how much you can learn, when you get together for a parent visit!

Of course, girl or boy, if you follow sports you can always talk about how your teams are doing, but what Dad or

Mom really want to learn from you is how *you* are doing, and who you are becoming.

You might want to take a tip from TV talk show hosts, too, and have a list of questions ready to ask your parent. Think of things you'd like to ask Dad (or Mom) and write them down. They might be about his new home — the house or apartment or the city or town — or about his job, his childhood, his side of the family, or anything else you'd like to ask. You can prepare a list of general discussion topics too, things that interest you, whether that's cars or sports, cooking or exploring, animals, coin collecting, or any of the topics mentioned earlier. And you also can prepare a list of things to tell Dad about yourself. Instead of telling him all the news over the phone, save a few items to tell him when you're together. (The lists are to remind yourself of things you want to tell him — not to *read* to him!)

Don't forget to be good listener, too. You'll probably want to hear how Dad is doing — although if he's really enjoying the peace and quiet of his own apartment, after all that fighting with Mom, you may not really be happy to hear that. And if he's been divorced for some time now, and he's starting to date other women, you probably don't want to hear that either! (And he really shouldn't tell you — unless you ask him straight out, or unless he's met someone really special and thinks she's going to be around in his life for a while.)

Making Yourself at Home

After your parents have been divorced (or at least separated) for a while, you'll get more used to going over to Dad or Mom's house to visit. The idea of one of your parents living somewhere else won't seem quite as strange. The house itself will become more familiar. And Mom won't feel that it's quite so urgent that she spend every minute with you, talking or doing something, when you go to her house.

Then you'll fall into a more comfortable routine, watching TV part of the time you're there, or reading, or doing your homework. You can talk on and off, when one of you thinks of something to say. You won't sit there staring at each other, knowing you're supposed to be talking to each other, yet unable to think of anything to talk about.

By then, too, you may start having friends come to visit you at Dad's or Mom's house. You don't want to spend all of your visiting weekend hanging with your friends. You're there to see your parent! But if a friend wants to spend a few hours with you, that would probably be fine. Depending on everyone's interests, you and your friend might even be able to do something together with your parent . . . going to a concert or show, playing miniature golf, bowling, shooting hoops, hiking, racing remote control cars, browsing at the flea market. . . .

To keep your dad's or mom's house from feeling quite so strange, and to keep you from feeling out of place there, it will help if you have a space of your own. The ideal thing would be for your dad's new house or apartment to have a room in it that's yours. Sometimes, though, that's not possible.

Your dad (or mom) may not be able to afford a two-bedroom place. Or he may have moved in with a friend or relative. Maybe he and his new roommate each have one bedroom, and there just isn't a third bedroom. In those cases, you may find yourself sleeping on a pull-out sofa in the living room, or in a second bed in your dad's bedroom. Or if Dad has moved in with a friend or relative who lives with his own child, your bed at your dad's might be a second bed in the room of the friend's child. The possible arrangements are endless, some good, some not so.

Hopefully, if you don't have a room of your own at the new home of the parent you live with only part-time, you at least have a bed of your own and a place to store your stuff. This may be a dresser and closet, part of a closet and two or three drawers in a dresser, or a large cabinet. Whatever space you can agree on signals to you that you belong there, that you have either your own room, or your own area . . . some space in the house that's *yours*.

You can keep things in your room, or your dresser, or your drawers. You can bring videogames, other games, books, CDs, or other stuff that's important to you, as well as clothing, a toothbrush, and other personal-care items, to leave at your mom or dad's house for the times you stay there. This will minimize the amount of stuff you have to carry back and forth; but even more importantly, it will give you the feeling of putting down some roots in that place; it will give you a sense of familiarity and comfort; it will make you feel more like you *belong* there.

If one parent has moved out of town, the scenario will be a little different. Let's assume you're living with Dad and visiting Mom. You probably will go to see Mom over your school's Christmas and/or Easter break, and for some part of the summer. This will make her house feel a little stranger to you, since you won't be spending time there on a regular basis.

If it's your dad and you who have moved away, while your mom has remained behind in your old hometown, then at least her *town* will be familiar even if she lives in a different house. If it's Mom who has moved, while you and Dad stayed behind, then the city she lives in will be as strange to you as the house itself.

If you're coming back to see Mom in your old hometown, you'll want to see your friends too, and after you've spent some time with Mom, she'll certainly understand if you want to visit your old friends. If you're going to see her in a new city, though, you probably won't know anyone there. (One exception to this is if Mom has moved back home to *her* old hometown, where part of her family still lives. Then visiting Mom might mean seeing Grandma and Grandpa, Aunt Liz, Uncle Ralph, Cousin Sean. . . .)

If your mom is living in a new town, and you don't know much about it, you can have a good time when Mom takes you around and shows you the sights.

Wherever Mom (or Dad) lives, when you go to visit, it's up to both of you to make you comfortable. You can help things along by bringing things to do so you don't get bored. Also, if you know that the visits are likely to be awkward at first, you'll be prepared for that, and it won't throw you for a loop. But remember, your mom may feel just as awkward as you do! That's right — she isn't used to having you as a visitor in her home! Just like you, she's used to having the two of you living under the same roof.

When you're going to spend time with a parent who lives a distance away from where you live, be prepared to be alone some time and bring stuff with you that you enjoy doing. Dad (or Mom) will probably have a TV set, but you may not have access to a computer, game system, a basketball hoop (or ball), or neighbor kids close to your age. Pack your own entertainment — books, cards, MP3 player, your journal, a camera — so you aren't bored.

Your non-custodial parent may live around the corner or across town—or she/he may live halfway across the continent. We'll talk about that possibility in the next chapter.

Points to Remember

• Most frequently in a divorce, the kids will live with their mother, but the kids will often live with Dad. Sometimes each parent gets one or more kids living with him or her. And some divorce courts award joint custody in a way that calls for the children to live part-time with each parent.

• One parent might move out of town.

• Some judges will pay attention to the wishes of a kid who's old enough and has a preference for living with one parent or the other.

• There are plenty of reasons why a parent who loves you very much might still think it's not a good idea for you to live with him or her.

• It can feel very awkward to try to talk to the parent you don't usually live with. Conversation may not feel at all natural, so give some thought to topics to discuss when you're together.

• Just the idea of "visiting your parent" will be strange too, at first.

• It helps if you have a room of your own, or at least a bed and some dresser drawers and closet space of your own, at your non-custodial parent's.

• Pack books, videogames, or other stuff to do before you go to visit your non-custodial parent.

• Take an active part in making yourself comfortable in both your parents' homes. It's not their job to entertain you, and you'll have a lot more fun-and a lot better relationship — if you meet them halfway!

"What's New
With You, Dad?"

▼ ▼ ▼

*Paul's parents divorced when he was in eighth grade.
It was early in November, and Paul thought to himself
that he sure didn't have anything to be thankful for
this Thanksgiving. At first, when Paul's dad moved out
of the house, he moved into a little apartment that he
rented by the month. He stayed there while he and
Paul's mom went through all the legal formalities,
getting the divorce agreement worked out, finalizing
everything. He stayed there for a little while longer
after that, but then he announced that he had had a
job offer that was too good to turn down. The
problem was, it was in New York; Paul and his family
lived in Illinois.*

*Paul's dad moved to New York, staying in a hotel
till he found an apartment. When Christmas vacation
started, Dad had not yet found one and was still
staying in the hotel. Since Paul's dad had just started*

the new job, he couldn't ask for time off to spend with Paul while he visited. There would be nothing for Paul to do all day in the hotel. And as a further complication, it was now so close to Christmas that there were no reasonably priced airline tickets available. So Paul didn't get to see his dad that Christmas.

By Easter break, though, Dad was living in a garden apartment in nearby New Jersey. In his phone calls, he described the apartment to Paul. It had just one bedroom, but the living room was L-shaped, and the alcove had a sliding partition that could close and make the area private. There was a futon in there that would be Paul's bed. The alcove would be his bedroom when he visited. (And it even had a cool name!)

At first, Paul was excited. At last he was going to see his dad again! And he was going to finally see New York City! He had always wanted to go to New York. His dad had promised to take one day off from work, and to take him into the city on both of the weekends Paul would be there. Maybe on an evening or two, Dad would come home from work, pick Paul up, and bring him back into the city to have dinner, or see a show, or see Chinatown, or something. There was so much to do in New York!

Paul arrived at Newark Airport on Friday evening. He scanned the crowd nervously for his dad. What if he wasn't here? What if he'd forgotten? What if he'd gotten a flat tire, or gotten hung up in traffic? Paul didn't know anyone in New York or New Jersey. But *there was Dad! Paul saw him and waved. He even ran to him. And Dad gave him a big, manly bearhug, squeezing the stuffing out of Paul, who came back with a bearhug of his own.*

Then, unaccountably, Paul felt awkward. This was a strange place to be with his dad. Dad should be home . . . in Paul's house. This was not a place he associated with his dad.

"How was the flight?" Dad asked. And Paul, who had flown only a couple of times before, and never alone, started talking about the flight, and that got them over the first awkward moments.

Talk of the flight, of the area they were driving through, of the apartment, and of what they would have for dinner occupied them all the way to the apartment. When they got there, Paul was amazed. Back home, he lived in a house. He had seen apartment buildings, of course, but they were different from this place, which was only two stories tall, had no elevator, looked newer than the apartment buildings back home, and was surrounded by a green, grassy area with bushes and flowers growing there.

It was when they got into the apartment that Paul was suddenly silenced.

Not that there was anything wrong with the place. It was clean and neat, and it had all the necessities. The alcove that was to be Paul's bedroom looked awfully small, though, and . . . well, the whole place was small. He couldn't imagine that this was his dad's home. It was tiny. Not a real house like they had always lived in. Where was the familiar furniture, or . . . well, the only thing he could see that looked like it really belonged to his dad was the mug sitting in the dish drain. It said WORLD'S GREATEST DAD. Paul had given it to Dad five years ago for Father's Day. Other than that, there wasn't a thing that Paul could recognize as his father's. Some total stranger might as well have lived there!

"Why don't you unpack and get comfortable?" Dad suggested. But comfortable was the last thing Paul felt. He wished he could turn around and go right back home!

"I thought I'd take you to this Italian place for dinner . . . but if you'd rather, there's Chinese. We're going to Chinatown in New York — the real stuff — one night soon, but if you want Chinese tonight too . . . or there's a nice restaurant a few blocks away . . . regular American food, but good. Maybe you'd rather . . . ?"

Dad's voice trailed off, and Paul realized that Dad was as uncomfortable as he was. And Paul was uncomfortable. Suddenly he didn't know what to say to Dad. His own father! He felt weird in this apartment. This wasn't his dad's home!

Things went from bad to worse when Dad said, "We're a little early for dinner. We can talk for a while before we go out. How are things at home?"

Suddenly Paul didn't know what to say. How were things at home? Should he tell about the nights he heard his mother crying behind her closed bedroom door? No! That wasn't right. Should he tell about how much he missed his dad? No. That might sound sappy.

Should he tell about his last three tests in school? No. He had already told his dad that on the phone. He had also told Dad about the way they'd given the substitute teacher a hard time, the way he'd gotten in a fight with Ian at school, the way he'd finally beaten Ron at the videogame that Ron beat everybody at. He'd told Dad about . . . he'd told Dad everything on the phone. There was nothing left to talk about. Except the way Mom cried, and that wasn't right to talk about.

"Everything's okay," Paul said, not really meaning it but not knowing what else to say. They sat there, staring at each other.

"Tell me about school," Dad finally said, and for a few minutes, Paul found a few things to tell Dad . . . but then he ran out of conversational tidbits, and once again they were staring at each other.

"What's new with you, Dad?" Paul finally asked.

Dad started talking about his job, but Paul didn't understand some of what Dad was talking about, and some of it was kind of boring. Finally, Dad said, "Well, I guess we can go to dinner." Paul was relieved.

They went to the Italian place. Paul had manicotti, and they compared the manicotti there with the manicotti back home. It was something to talk about. Dad had lasagna. He talked about learning how to make lasagna. He had never been interested in learning to cook lasagna before. Paul found himself wondering who had taught Dad. Was it some woman? Paul knew Dad might be dating women, but the thought made him very uncomfortable...as if Dad were being disloyal to Mom. Paul knew that Dad and Mom were divorced, and they were both free to date other people. But Mom wasn't dating any other guys. Dad shouldn't be dating any other women!

After dinner, they went back home. That's when things got really uncomfortable. They just sat there, staring at each other, trying to think of things to say to each other. Paul couldn't think of any news that he hadn't told Dad on the phone already. Dad couldn't think of anything to tell Paul that he hadn't already told him, either. They just looked at each other . . . and didn't know what to say.

Finally Paul said, "How about playing some kind of game?" But he hadn't brought any games with him, and Dad didn't have any there. Dad tried to ask Paul some questions to start a conversation going, but Paul felt awkward and strange, the unfamiliar surroundings didn't help, and he couldn't think of anything interesting to tell his dad that he hadn't already told him.

Finally Dad started telling Paul stories from his childhood, stories about Paul's grandma, uncle, aunt, and dad when they were all much younger. The stories were moderately interesting, and they did help to pass the time.

When Dad said, "You've had a long day. Suppose we go to bed early?" Paul didn't even object.

The next day was Saturday, and Dad took Paul into the city. They saw Rockefeller Center, went to the Radio City Music Hall, then headed downtown to Chinatown, where they ate a great meal. Heading back uptown, they walked around the Times Square area, where Paul got his first look at the theatre district. It was dark, and the theatre marquees were all lit. Paul was impressed. By the time they got home to New Jersey, it was pretty late. Paul and his dad had a soda and talked about all they'd seen in New York City.

The next day, they went back into the city, and Dad showed Paul the view of the city from the observation deck of the Empire State Building, then took him for a ride on the Staten Island ferry. After that, they rode the subways and buses, looking at lots of different neighborhoods. Paul was amazed at the many different kinds of areas that are all part of New York. They went to a huge store that sold music, and Dad gave Paul $50 to spend on CDs. They had dinner in a neighborhood restaurant on the Upper West Side, and Paul tried buffalo steak for the first time in his life.

When they got back to Dad's apartment building in New Jersey, there was a boy about Paul's age walking out front. Paul stopped to talk to him and found out his name was Jared. When Jared heard that Paul's dad had to work the next morning, he invited Paul to hang out with him. Jared had tons of video games and other neat stuff, so they got together a lot over the remaining week.

Monday night, when Dad came home from work, he told Paul about his day, and Paul told Dad the fun time he'd had with Jared. Then they threw together a batch of spaghetti and meatballs. Dinner was late, but good, and by the time they ran out of things to say to each other, it was nearly ten o'clock.

The next morning, Paul went into the city with Dad, looked around Dad's office, and then went out on his own exploring the area of the city nearby. They had lunch together, and then Paul took the bus back to New Jersey and hung out with Jared the rest of the afternoon. That night, Paul and Dad went out for pizza and took Jared with them. This made conversation even easier.

When they got back to Paul's dad's place, Jared went home, and Paul and Dad talked. Paul told Dad about his exploration of the area around Dad's office, and Dad told Paul a little of the history of New York. He talked about the people and the customs, instead of about the facts and figures that bored Paul in history class at school, so Paul found the conversation interesting. Soon it was bedtime.

The rest of the week went much smoother. Jared and Paul walked to a magazine shop, where Paul bought some car magazines, which he read when he was by himself, but he still spent a lot of time with Jared, too, Then, when he was with his dad, he told Dad what he and Jared had done, or what he'd read about in the magazines. They talked about cars, and about the car that Paul would like to own when he got his license.

Finally, they talked about how weird it felt to Paul to not have Dad at home. Paul felt more comfortable talking about this now. And when there were lulls in the conversation, silences when neither of them had anything to say, it didn't feel so uncomfortable and awkward.

On Saturday, they went back into the city again, and Dad showed Paul more sights, more neighborhoods, and more good places to eat. They had both lunch and dinner in the city, and then Dad took Paul to a Broadway show. It was a comedy that Paul thought was really good.

The next day, when Dad took Paul back to Newark Airport, Paul said, "I'm gonna miss you all over again! I can't wait till summer vacation!" And he meant it. The first day, he had wanted to go right back home, but now he was sorry to leave.

Next visit he would bring more things to do while he was on his own. Next visit, too, Dad would have some time off work for summer vacation and be able to spend more time with Paul. That would make things better as well. And Jared had said he'd be around during the summer. Dad had also promised to keep his eyes out for other kids Paul's age who might live in the apartment building.

It had turned out to be a good visit after all! Paul decided that having two "homes" might not be so bad.

▲ ▲ ▲

6

Parents at a Distance

Paul's visit to his dad in New York was quite a production, wasn't it? The flight, the small apartment, the awkward silences, wondering what to do, finding a new friend, visiting Dad's office. . . .

It's so much easier when Mom and Dad live near each other, and you can get back and forth between their houses easily. Maybe Mom drives you to Dad's or Dad picks you up at Mom's. Maybe you bike back and forth or take the city bus. If you're old enough to drive, you can even get yourself back and forth. But in any case, getting back and forth shouldn't be a major problem.

But what do you do when one parent or the other moves out of town? We talked a little about this earlier, but let's look at this situation more closely.

In an ideal world, divorcing parents would both remain in the same town till their kids were grown, to make it easier for the kids to be close to both parents. But this isn't an ideal world, and sometimes people need to move.

What are some of the reasons parents move? A parent may be transferred by the company for which he or she works. Parents may get better job offers, with salary increases so big they can't afford not to take it. Parents sometimes lose their jobs — and the only good job may be in another town. A parent may need to move to be near a sick relative.

If Mom's mom, who lives alone in Dubuque, gets seriously ill with something long-term, Mom may need to move to Dubuque to be near Grandma and help take care of her. On the other hand, it may be Mom who needs the help. Sometimes a custodial parent needs to move near her (or his) mother or sister or other relative in order to have help raising the kids. If you're in high school, and you're an only child, this probably isn't an issue, but suppose you're thirteen, and you have a ten-year-old sister and a six-year-old brother. Mom may need to move near Grandma or Aunt Ellie in order to have some help with the kids, especially if she was a stay-at-home mom till the divorce and now needs to go back to work.

There are other reasons to move, too. One is simply for a fresh start. After a divorce, some people like to get a new start in a new place . . . perhaps one where the neighbors aren't gossiping about the divorce. Another reason may be climate. A man or woman who hates the cold weather — or who loves to ski — may have been married to someone who didn't feel the same way, or who couldn't move because of his or her job. Now, divorced, this person is able to move to the warmth of Arizona, Florida, or California, or to a ski area such as Canada, Colorado, or Vermont. A friendlier community is another good reason to move. A newly divorced person may simply want to move back to his home town, where he feels more at ease.

Keeping in Touch

Of course, if your mom or dad moved after the divorce, and they now live a considerable distance from each other, you won't get to see your non-custodial parent as often as if Mom and Dad simply lived across town from each other. But you know you'll get to see Dad (or Mom, if you live mostly with Dad) *sometimes* — probably during most or all of the long school breaks such as Christmas, Easter, and summer. We've discussed this already in another chapter. But it's also important to think about keeping in touch between visits.

The easiest and least expensive way to talk to each other is via email or IM (Instant Messaging). Assuming you each already have a computer and an email service, you can send as many emails to each other as you want. And if you both have the same Instant Messaging software, you can IM each other, too. (If by any chance you both have webcams, you can see each other while you IM.)

If Dad doesn't have email, you can still send old-fashioned "snailmail" (postal mail) letters back and forth, though they'll take longer to arrive. But snailmail is good for sending Dad such things as a photocopy of that essay you got a 97 on, pictures that aren't digital, a copy of the program from the school chorus concert in which you sang the solo (and maybe a tape or CD or MD recording), or a copy of the article in the local paper about how your basket just before the final buzzer saved the game for your team.

And for the comforting sound of your faraway parent's voice, there's nothing like a phone call. Of course, long distance calls cost money, but if you keep the calls short enough, the cost shouldn't be too severe. And your distant parent can get a "personal 800 number" — like the 800 number businesses have — which allows for a person to call long distance without it costing anything. (The person receiving the call — your dad, if you're calling him — pays the cost.) This way your mom can't complain that you're spending too much money calling Dad.

If you or a friend own a video camera, you can have a friend make videotapes of you to send, so Mom/Dad can see how you look now. You can show off your new muscles or new clothes. If you're an athlete, you might want your friend to photograph you in action on the basketball court, football field, soccer field, or whatever is applicable. If you're a performer — if you're a singer, dancer, or actor, or if you play an instrument — you can perform on tape, so your parent can watch and listen. If you're on the cheerleading squad, you can perform a few cheers.

And you can simply talk. If you're comfortable with it, just face the camera, pretend you're looking at your mom or dad, and just talk to her/him. Or you and a friend — either the one who's holding the camera or a third friend — can pretend the friend is interviewing you, the way they do on TV. The interviewer can ask you questions, ranging from whether you've gotten any good grades in school lately to questions about your hobbies, your other interests (including sports or performing), or new things you've recently learned. Plan it with your friend in advance, so that the questions help you to give answers that will provide the info you want your remote parent to have or think she'll enjoy hearing.

The interview doesn't have to be what TV professionals call "talking heads" — all talk and no action. If you've recently caught an impressive fish, you can show it or, if it's already filleted and in your freezer, you can show on a yardstick just how long it measured. If you've recently redecorated or rearranged your room, you can take a video tour of the room, showing off the new look. If you've learned how to quilt, knit, or do woodworking or metalwork, you can display some of your recently finished work.

You can't get a hug long-distance, but you don't have to be out of touch!

Points to Remember

• Sometimes one parent or the other moves out of town. It may be the parent you live with most of the time, or the other one.

• There are many reasons a parent might move. Some of these have to do with the divorce. Some don't.

• If one of your parents moves away, or if you move with one parent, you can still spend time with the other parent on school vacations.

• Bring things with you to keep yourself entertained when the parent you're visiting is working or busy.

• You can keep in touch between visits by email, IM, snailmail, webcam, videotapes, audiotapes, and long-distance calls.

7

Unfair Tactics

Your parents don't mean to be unfair, but they're human.
And, being human, they have their faults like everyone else.
There are two things that divorced parents sometimes ask of
their children that are totally unfair. One is to carry
messages, and the other is to supply unreasonable
information.

What am I talking about? I'll explain.

Unfair Tactic #1: The Messenger

Let's start with carrying messages. When Mom and Dad no
longer talk to each other comfortably — as often happens
after a divorce — they may want to have as little to do with
each other as possible. This can even include avoiding the
shortest of phone calls. Mom and Dad may still be upset
with each other over the issues that caused them to get the
divorce in the first place. They may be angry over things
that were said, or demands that were made, during the
divorce proceedings. If only one parent wanted the divorce,

the other one may be angry or hurt, or both, at the one who started this whole ball rolling. Or they may simply feel too awkward, after the divorce, to talk to each other comfortably. So they may avoid talking to each other . . . even briefly, and even on the phone.

Now, suppose Mom's sister Ilene is having a family birthday party in two weeks, and it's a day when you're supposed to be at Dad's. Mom may want to trade weekends with Dad so that you're able to go to Aunt Ilene's party. But she may not want to call Dad and have to talk to him about it.

She might ask you, "Please tell Dad that Aunt Ilene's 40th birthday party is in two weeks, and I'd like you to go. Ask Dad if he can trade weekends with me. You could visit him again next weekend and stay here the weekend after that. Okay?"

You might say, "Okay," thinking it's no problem to ask Dad such a simple thing. But really, it's not okay. Of course, Dad might just say yes, and then it's settled, but chances are that there'll be more to it than that. Maybe Dad is willing to let you go to Aunt Ilene's party, but next weekend doesn't work for him. Or maybe he has plans for you for that Sunday, and he's okay with your staying home to go to Aunt Ilene's party on Saturday, but he wants you at his house on Sunday. This is beginning to get complicated, and Dad and Mom really need to work this out between themselves and get it straightened out and set up definitely.

Or maybe Dad thinks Mom is switching days with him too often, and he wants her to know how he feels. He certainly shouldn't tell *you* that he resents her taking advantage of him, if that's how he feels about it. Neither should you have to carry that message back to Mom and tell her. If they have anything negative to say about each other, they should say it directly — you *certainly* shouldn't be the messenger for that kind of message!

Mom and Dad should work out plans for your visits themselves, though they ought to check with you, too, just to make sure you don't have any kind of conflict before they switch the schedule. You should be out of the middle of such message carrying.

Even worse is when Mom asks you to tell Dad, "The child support check is late," or when Dad asks you to tell Mom, "I don't approve of the way Jennifer is dressing. Why do you let her wear those kinds of clothes?" or when Mom asks you to carry a message such as, "Mom says if you hadn't spent so much money on a sports car, you'd have been able to chip in toward my class trip to Washington."

If Mom and Dad have messages for each other, they need to pick up the phone and tell each other directly — even if the message is innocent and pleasant. And if Mom or Dad asks you to carry a message from one to the other, you have every right to refuse. You can politely but firmly say, "That's not appropriate for me to tell Dad. You need to tell him yourself," or "That's not the right thing for me to tell Mom. Please call her so you can tell her yourself."

Even worse are "sneaky" messages. These are messages one parent asks you to deliver to the other without it being apparent you were asked to deliver the message. An example would be the father who tells his visiting daughter, "Make sure Mom knows I haven't been dating anyone," or the mother who tells her son, before he goes to visit his father, "Try to let Dad know that you know I'm not happy." Other messages you shouldn't be asked to carry include ones like, "Make sure and tell Dad how tight we are for money. Tell him you hate eating pasta or bean soup three nights a week — you'd like some meat, if only I could afford to buy it."

You shouldn't carry messages. (You shouldn't be *asked* to carry messages; but parents are human, so of course they sometimes say or do things they shouldn't.) If either of your parents asks you to carry a message, you have every right to politely but firmly decline. Refuse. Say, "I'm sorry, Mom, but this is between you and Dad. I shouldn't be in the middle. Please call him and tell him yourself." Or "I'm sorry, Dad, but Mom gets upset when you send these messages. If I deliver the message, she gets upset with me. And that's not fair to me, is it? This is between you and Mom. Please don't make me get caught in the middle."

Remember, you have a right to say no to carrying messages.

Unfair Tactic #2: The Spy

But parents don't just ask their kids to play the part of messengers. They also ask them to play the part of spies. And that's even worse.

▼ ▼ ▼

Steffi's parents had been divorced for four months now. It had been a difficult divorce, full of bad feelings, and neither her mom nor her dad wanted to talk to each other, though both were very curious about what was going on in each other's life.

When Steffi got to her dad's new apartment, she put her backpack and bag in her room, then went to

the fridge. "What do you have that I can eat?" she
asked.

"It's almost lunchtime. Why don't you wait? We can
eat in half an hour or so. Talk to me. Tell me what's
going on at home," Dad said.

Steffi started to tell Dad her news of the week, but
he seemed distracted, like he was only half listening.
Finally he asked her, "And what do you and Mom do
in the evenings?"

"The same as always," Steffi answered.

"Does Mom get bored staying home alone all
evening . . . or doesn't she stay alone all evening?"

Steffi didn't know where this conversation was
headed, but she felt vaguely uncomfortable about it.
"Sometimes," she answered noncomittally.

"Where does she go?" Dad asked.

"Oh . . . you know. To a friend's, sometimes."

"Do her friends come to the house?"

"Sometimes."

"Does she have any new friends?" Steffi noticed that
her dad's voice sounded kind of nervous. She
shrugged her shoulders without saying anything.

"Well, who comes over to the house?" Steffi's dad
asked.

Steffi shrugged again. Her dad stared at her. "You
know," Steffi said with another shrug. "Her friends.
Whoever. I don't know."

"Are any of them men?"

Steffi said, "Well, Evan, Chuck, David, and Bert
and . . . you know. . . . " She was naming the
husbands of her mother's friends.

"Any new ones? New friends? Friends who don't have wives? Or are Evan and Chuck and David and Bert coming over by themselves?" Dad's tone grew sharp.

Steffi sounded nervous when she answered. She didn't know what this conversation was about, but she knew it was making her uncomfortable. "Well, Bert came over without Carole when he fixed the kitchen light for Mom, and Chuck came over without Renee when the disposer broke down. And Renee came over without Chuck when Mom needed help with a sewing pattern."

"That's not what I asked you."

"Why are you asking me these questions, Dad?"

"I'm just making conversation. I'm just wondering what's going on back home . . . I mean, back in your home. That's all!" Dad's tone sounded very sharp.

"Do you want help fixing lunch?" Steffi asked, getting up from the chair.

"Yes, thanks," Dad said, getting up too and walking to the fridge. And for the moment the interrogation was over, but Steffi was in for the other half when she got home to her mom's house Sunday evening.

"How is your dad?" Mom asked.

"Fine," Steffi said.

"Does he seem happy?" Mom asked.

"I don't know," Steffi answered, curling a long strand of hair tightly around her finger.

"Has he bought any new furniture? Does the place look any different?"

"He's always getting new stuff. Every time I go there. But he still needs a lot more things."

"Do his new things look like he picked them out?" Mom asked.

"I don't know!" Steffi answered, sighing in exasperation. "How am I supposed to know if Dad picked out a chair or a vase?"

"He has a new vase?" Mom's head whipped around sharply. "Did you notice anything different in his closet? Any women's clothes?"

"I wasn't in Dad's closet," Steffi said. "Why would I be in Dad's closet?"

"I don't know!" Mom snapped. "Don't you pay attention to things?"

"I think you and Dad pay too much attention to things!" Steffi snapped back. Then she left the room, went into her room, and closed the door. She supposed she'd get a lecture later about being fresh to her mother, but she had had it with all the questions, first from her dad and then from her mom. What did they want to know, anyhow? What were all these questions about? And why were they still so interested in each other if they no longer loved each other and didn't want to be married to each other? Steffi thought she'd never understand her parents!

▲ ▲ ▲

Divorced parents often wonder what's going on in their ex-spouses' lives. Sometimes the questions are based simply on curiosity and nothing more. Sometimes questions come up when one parent is late paying child support to the other or says he can't help with extra money for an unexpected need like braces for Vic's teeth or to send Shauna to volleyball camp. The other parent — usually the mother — may wonder if Dad is really that broke, or if he has plenty of money for his own needs. So she'll ask her child questions such as whether Dad has new furniture, new clothes, or a new car.

Sometimes questions are based on jealousy. Dad and Mom may each wonder if the other is dating anyone yet. Dad might ask if any new men are coming to visit. Mom might ask if there are any signs of women's clothing around Dad's house, or even how many toothbrushes there are in Dad's bathroom. Like Steffi's mom, Mom might also try to find out if Dad's house looks like some woman has been helping to make the house look nicer.

They may also ask questions designed to find out whether the other is doing a good job as a parent: "What does Dad feed you when you're at his house?" "Does Mom keep the house clean?"

Not all questions are bad. "Does Dad see that you get your homework done when you're at his house?" is a fair question. "Is it warm enough at Dad's house, or do you need to bring along an extra sweater?" is also all right.

But if there's anything Mom wants to find out from Dad, anything Dad wants to tell Mom, let them communicate directly. They should leave you out of the middle, just as with message-carrying.

It's not fair for Mom or Dad to ask you play spy. You shouldn't be put in that position. And you have every right to refuse. You can tell them, "You're asking me to play favorites. If I spy on one of you and not the other, I'm playing favorites between my two parents. And if I spy on both of you . . . well, do you want me telling Mom/Dad all about what *you're* doing? So please, stop asking me those kinds of questions."

You *do* have the right to refuse to carry a message or to play spy.

Points to Remember

• Divorced parents are often curious about what's going on in each other's life.

• Divorced parents sometimes are uncomfortable talking to each other, even briefly, even just by phone.

• It's not fair for your parents to ask you to carry messages to each other. *You have the right to refuse.*

• It's also not fair for them to ask you to spy on each other. *You have the right to refuse.*

8

A Time of Turmoil

The dictionary defines "turmoil" as "an extremely confused or agitated condition" — and isn't that the perfect definition of the condition a teenager (or any kid) would be in after learning that his or her parents are getting divorced?

When your life is being uprooted all around you, and your mind is in an uproar, it's not really easy to think clearly. And when people — people of any age, not just kids — are in a state of turmoil, they're more likely to have trouble thinking clearly. They're more likely to make bad decisions.

So part of this short chapter isn't specifically about your parents' divorce. Instead, it's about avoiding the kinds of mistakes you might be likely to make. It's about making good decisions instead of bad ones.

Decisions, Decisions

What are some of the bad decisions you might be tempted to make?

• Someone might offer you drugs. Normally you'd say no to drugs, but because you can't think clearly, and/or because you're hurting in your heart or messed-up in your head, suddenly "escaping" your problems through drugs seems like a tempting idea. Or because your whole life feels like it's falling apart, you might think, *What's the difference? Everything's all ruined in my life anyhow.* And you could be tempted to say yes.

• Your boyfriend (or girlfriend) might pressure you for sex. Up till now, perhaps you've had a G-rated — or at most an R-rated — relationship with him or her, but now you feel as if it doesn't matter if you give in. Your whole life feels ruined anyway, so what's the difference?! Or you feel that this is the one person who loves you and is still there for you, so why shouldn't you get even closer to her or him?

• A friend asks you to help him cheat on a test. You normally wouldn't do that. Not only is it ethically wrong, but you might get caught and get in trouble! But now, with your whole world in turmoil, little things like right and wrong, or the fear of getting caught, seem less important. Or maybe you just can't think clearly. Why shouldn't you help a friend who has helped you? (This is especially true if it's a friend who has helped you get through all the upset of your parents' divorce, and now the friend says, "I was there for you when you needed me. You owe me one.")

• A friend asks you to lend him your car. You know he's not a good driver, or you know he sometimes has a few beers and then drives. Or maybe he's a good, safe, responsible driver, but your parents have explicitly forbidden you to lend the car to anyone. But what your parents want doesn't seem so important now . . . after all, they're messing up your happiness, aren't they? What's it going to hurt to lend your friend the car?

• A friend who smokes asks you to buy cigarettes for her. You're not old enough and neither is she, but you look older than your age, so maybe they won't ID you. "It can't hurt to try," she says. "What's the worst they can do? Refuse to sell them to you?" You know it's not healthy for your friend to smoke — but you also know she's going to get those cigarettes somehow or other. It's not like you're turning her on to cigarettes for the first time. She's already smoking. The damage is done. You also know it's not right for you to buy cigarettes when you're underage. But you just don't care.

• A friend offers to get you fake ID so you can buy beer or vodka or wine coolers any time you want. Your friend does it all the time and gets away with it. Why shouldn't you?

• Your mom asks you to try to find out if your dad got that raise, or even to try to look at his checkbook and find out how much money he has. Or maybe the request is for information that's a little less sensitive. Maybe she "only" asks you to try to find out if he's dating anyone yet, or to let her know if there is an additional toothbrush in his bathroom that might belong to a woman. Or perhaps your dad asks you to carry messages to your mom. "Tell your mother that I don't appreciate her going out so many evenings. She needs to stay home with you more." Or "Tell your mother that I want her to spend the child support money on *you*. I don't like the idea that she's driving around in a new car that I've paid for." What do you care if they send messages to each other through you, or find out about each other's private lives by making you the spy?

• You might be tempted to sneak into the movies, or to try to get in to see a movie rated for age seventeen and older, though you're not yet that old. You might be tempted to shoplift. Should you do it? When your world feels like it's falling apart, it's easy to be reckless. When it seems no one is treating you fairly, it's harder to remember that you need to play fair with others, and to make good moral/ethical decisions.

• Even your everyday decisions can be affected by the state of mind you're in as a result of being upset by your parents' divorce. I'm talking about deciding whether to do your homework first or blow it off till later and spend time playing videogames first. I'm talking about deciding what to eat when you're on your own for dinner. Should you have a cheeseburger and fries, or chicken and salad?

How to Make Good Decisions

So . . . what should you do? All of these situations call for decision-making. And your decision-making processes are certainly likely to be clouded by the state you're in.

You need to mentally take a step back and distance yourself from the problem or question. Then try to answer each of the following questions in your head (or on paper):

1. What is the problem you're facing, or the question you need to answer or decision you need to make?

2. What are the possible solutions to the problem, or answers to the question, or decisions you could choose?

3. For each of the possible solutions or answers or decisions, what are the good points in its favor? What good things could happen as a result of your making that choice?

4. For each of the possible solutions or decisions, what are the bad points against it? What bad things could happen as a result of your making that choice?

5. Is there *another* alternative you hadn't yet thought of?

When you have these questions all answered, you should be able to make a good decision more easily.

If you can't seem to reach a decision on your own, you can always look for advice or input from someone else. Who that someone else is will depend in part on what the question or problem is. People you might go to include:

• **A friend** who is level-headed and sensible, whose opinions you trust.

• **A relative you're close to** — perhaps an aunt, uncle, grandparent, or older cousin. Or maybe you have an older sister or brother, already grown, whom you're close to.

• **The school guidance counselor.**

• **The youth group leader or clergyperson from a religious organization.**

• **A favorite teacher or coach** whose opinion you value.

• **A parent of one of your friends** — an adult you're close to, can talk to, and whose thinking you respect.

If you think you can't trust your own judgment at this time in your life, don't be afraid to ask for help or input. There's no shame in asking for advice. People of all ages do it every day. You don't need someone to tell you what to do; you need someone who'll help you decide for yourself. Often just talking it out — just using someone else as a sounding board — will help you make the best decision.

If it's a situation where a quick decision is needed, and you have no time to get help from anyone else, run down that checklist in your mind, think about the possible results — short-term and long-term — of saying yes or no to the friend who wants to borrow your car or the friend who wants you to buy cigarettes for her or whatever, and then do what you feel in your heart is really right — the situation with the best outcome for you.

Just don't use "it doesn't matter to me anymore" as an excuse to make careless decisions. It *will* matter to you tomorrow.

Points to Remember

• It's easy to make bad decisions when your head is messed up over something as unsettling as a divorce. This applies both to decisions about things that have to do with your parents and their divorce, and decisions in general.

• It helps to go through a decision-making process, asking yourself certain questions that will help you come to a good decision.

• If there's time — if it's not a decision you have to make on the spot — there are people you can go to for help in making decisions.

• There's no shame in asking for help with decision-making.

• If you do seek help from someone else, you don't have to follow their advice. Let them help you make your own choice.

Remember that the decision you make today will matter to you tomorrow.

9

The FAQ Chapter

This chapter may seem a bit long. Feel free to skip over any questions that don't seem to apply to you. But keep in mind that reading about other people's issues can help you keep things in perspective.

Q: *I saw a movie called* The Parent Trap. *In it, some kids got their divorced parents back together. How can I make that happen in real life?*

A: In real life — unlike the Hollywood version — the best thing is not to try. You probably don't know all of the reasons your parents broke up. Even if you know that they argued all the time, you don't know whether most of the arguments centered around a deeper underlying problem. It may not be that they simply couldn't get along. There may be a more fundamental reason. Or the constant arguing may not have been the real reason they broke up. Instead, they may have had another, larger problem, and as a result of the bad feelings they had for each other due to that problem, they picked on each other. It may not be as simple as, "If they could learn to stop fighting, they could get along."

And of course, it may not be at all a case of their arguing and simply not getting along. One of them may have done something that the other one cannot forgive. One of them may have done something that caused the other to feel he or she can no longer trust him or her. Or one or both may simply no longer feel love for the other. Though parents never stop loving their kids, husbands and wives can stop loving each other. Sometimes people change so much that one says to the other, "You're so different from the way you used to be. You're not the person I fell in love with and married." An industrious person can become lazy. A thoughtful person can become thoughtless. A neat person can become a slob. A generous person can become stingy. A funny person can become ultra-serious. A person who liked to spend time with other people can become quiet and withdrawn.

Some problems between couples can be worked out, often with the help of a marriage counselor or other professional. Some problems go beyond what a professional can help solve, especially if one partner has changed radically, or if one partner is no longer interested in keeping the marriage together.

If there were a chance that marriage counseling could help your parents' marriage, they probably have already tried it.

So, since you don't know the full story behind your parents' divorce, don't try to "play adhesive" and glue them back together. It almost never works out.

Q: *I don't think Dad wanted the divorce, just Mom. Does that mean there's a better chance of them getting back together?*

A: Some couples do try a second time, and some even have better results the second time; but unless the underlying problems are solved, nothing will be different the second time around. My best friend's parents got divorced, and her mom married someone else. Later she divorced this man and eventually remarried her first husband. But the same problems that troubled their first marriage were still there, and eventually they got divorced again.

It's possible that your mom will decide she's sorry she got divorced. But it's not likely. And even if it happens, that's no guarantee they'll stay married. Unless they overcome whatever was wrong with the marriage to begin with, the second try isn't likely to work out any better than the first. So please don't get your hopes up.

Q: *Mom is sad all the time since Dad moved out. What's a good way to help her feel better?*

A: Be a loving son or daughter to her. Help her around the house when you can. Be thoughtful — ask what you can do to make her feel better, pick her a bouquet of wildflowers, make her favorite dinner if you're any kind of cook. (And the only way you'll get to be any kind of cook is to *cook!*) Put your head together with her best friend and plan a surprise party for her next birthday, or for no occasion at all. Be considerate and don't give her unnecessary problems. This isn't the time she needs to worry because you're an hour late coming home or you're hanging out with a bad crowd.

But if you don't succeed in making her happier, don't feel bad about it. Remember, *you're not responsible for your mother's happiness.*

Q: *I know my mom was the one who wanted the divorce, but now she doesn't seem very happy. Why would she ask for a divorce if it's just going to make her sad?*

A: Do you know the expression, "the lesser of two evils"? She may have felt it was necessary to get a divorce for some reason that you don't know. Now that she's gotten the divorce, she probably remembers how things used to be, early in the marriage, before things went wrong. And she may wish she could go back to the way things used to be — which, in most cases, isn't possible. This would make her sad.

Or she may simply be lonely, or overwhelmed with work and responsibilities, or troubled by money worries.

In each of these cases, she might very well feel sad, or overburdened. That doesn't mean she'd like to be married to your dad again; it just means that the alternative — being divorced — isn't necessarily easy either. But it's not as bad as being married and putting up with whatever situation caused her to ask for the divorce in the first place.

Q: *My parents say they're "separated." What's the difference between "separated" and "divorced"? It feels like a divorce to me.*

A: There are two kinds of separation. One is a "trial separation." A couple that enters into a trial separation is trying to see if living separately is better than living together in a marriage that's not working well. After they've lived apart for a month or three or six, they may decide that being married to each other is better after all, despite their problems. Or they may feel a sense of relief at being shed of the problems that existed in the marriage, and they may decide that, yes, they do want to get divorced.

The other kind of separation isn't a trial; it's a step before getting divorced. The couple has definitely decided to divorce, but the lawyers are still hammering out the terms of the divorce. It isn't final yet. Both partners definitely intend to get divorced though. Till the judge grants the divorce decree, they're not formally divorced, but they're on their way. They're *separated*. They've broken up, and they're only waiting for the legalities to make it official. (There's more about separations later in this chapter.)

Q: *How old do you have to be before the judge will let you live with the parent you want to live with?*

A: There's no hard-and-fast rule to answer this with. There's not one set age at which a judge automatically listens to a son or daughter who has a preference. It depends on many things. Your state's law may control it. Your age is a factor, your maturity level (regardless of your age) is one, the judge's own beliefs are another, and the circumstances surrounding the divorce are still another. Let's say you want to go live with your dad. If your mom and dad agree to that, there's a very good chance the judge will agree too. If your mom doesn't agree, the judge will have to make the decision.

Suppose your dad works mostly at home. This might sway the judge toward letting you live with your dad (though it's not a guarantee). But, at the other extreme, if your dad works two shifts and is home very little, the judge is much less likely to agree. Other things could sway the judge against agreeing to your dad having custody. For example, if your dad has a criminal record, is in treatment for substance abuse, or has serious health problems, this could weigh against the possibility of your being allowed to live with him.

But if you're a teenager, the judge probably will give some consideration to your wishes, even though he or she doesn't necessarily have to abide by them.

Q: *The judge set up a visiting schedule for when I can see my dad. Why can't I see him more often?*

A: If your mom, your dad, and you all agree to it, you can see him more often. The visiting schedule doesn't need to be rigid. If your dad wants to see you, you want to see him, and it's a scheduled visiting day, your mom doesn't have the right to refuse to let you go to his house. (Of course, if you're sick with something more than just the sniffles, she has a right to keep you home.) If it's not a scheduled visiting day, your mom has the right to keep you home. But if she wants to let you go to your dad's, it's okay with your dad, and it's not going to interfere with getting your homework and chores done, your parents can work out extra visiting time for you.

Q: *My brother went to live with Dad after the divorce, but I'm still living in the old house with Mom. My brother has it better because he has his own room (while I have to share with my sister), Dad's a good cook (Mom's cooking is awful), and Dad's easier to live with than Mom is. How do I convince Mom to let me move in with Dad?*

A: Well, not by telling her that Dad's easier to live with or that her cooking is awful! I'll answer your question in a minute, but first let me bring up a few points.

Any kid who wants to live with the other parent needs to stop and consider some things. First of all, *why* does she (or he) want to move? Is the parent she lives with now really difficult to live with — or is it just that she thinks the other one will be less strict? Would living with the other parent really be an improvement — or does it just seem that way because there are disciplinary hassles at home, hassles that would occur with either parent? Would life really be better with the other parent — or does the other one simply have a nicer house or live nearer to the mall or school or the gym or something like that?

Are you sure there's a place for you at your other parent's house? Does Dad have a third bedroom so you'd have your own room like your brother does? Are you sure your other parent is prepared to have you live with him or her? Are you sure the situation where you are now can't be improved? Whether it's a matter of having to share a room, or some other problem, if you made your mom (in this case) aware of how important it is to you, maybe she'd do something about it. (Maybe she can't, but it's worth asking.)

Or maybe the real reason a teenager wants to move out of her mom's house and into her dad's is something different . . . maybe even something the teen isn't aware of herself. If it's that Mom has been depressed since the divorce, this is a temporary situation. It *will* get better. (And right now, your being there will help Mom.)

Or maybe the divorce took place a year ago, Mom's dating now, and you don't like her new boyfriend, who's around a lot. Is he really unkind, or icky, or otherwise unpleasant? Or is it just that he's not Dad? If it's just that he's not Dad, that's not a good reason to move. If he's truly unlikable, you may have a good reason to want to move out. But don't tell Mom, "Robert's a loser!" Just say you're not comfortable around him. (Of course, if he's done anything really wrong to you, *you need to tell your mom* — or another trusted adult — about that.)

And have you thought about how you're going to ask the parent you're living with now about moving out? You probably don't want to hurt anyone's feelings!

Now let's look at the specific situation raised in your question, and I'll give you those answers I promised.

You could try asking Mom to let you live with Dad for a few months to see how you like it. She might agree; she might not. But it's worth trying. Try coming up with a persuasive reason, though — one that won't hurt Mom's feelings.

You might even find, after you try it for a few months, that living with Dad isn't everything you thought it would be. But, since you're putting it in terms of "trying it out," rather than flat-out "moving," you won't have slammed any doors behind you. You'll be able to move back into Mom's house if you find that, after all, living with Mom was better than you thought.

One other thought: Have you thought about what *you* could do to make life better in your mom's house? How about learning to cook and doing some of the meals yourself? Could you get along better with Mom if you changed some things: your communication with her, your willingness to pitch in, your attitude?

Q: *My parents have been divorced almost a year now. At first, Dad saw me all the time, but now he's often "too busy" or has "something else" he has to do. Is there any way I can get him to see me more often?*

A: The first thing to do is talk to him and tell him how much you miss him. Parents are humans just like kids — and are just as likely to mess up because of their own needs.

Of course you want to see him more often. He's your dad! It's normal for there to be an occasional week when he's genuinely too busy to see you. (Or when you're really too busy to see him.) Lots of things can get in the way. He might have a business meeting or need to be out of town. You might have a school sports event. But if it's happening a lot, I suspect something else is stopping your dad from seeing you.

Although it must hurt, please understand that the greatest likelihood is that it's got nothing to do with you. (One exception to this would be if you're making the visits uncomfortable. Have you been putting pressure on Dad to "come home," or criticizing his new girlfriend, or acting sullen or argumentative? If you have, maybe your dad's had enough of it. But if not, it's pretty safe to assume it's nothing you've done!)

There are many possible reasons for your dad's reluctance to see you as often as he might. If your mom now has a new husband (or a boyfriend who's around often), Dad may not be comfortable coming to pick you up at Mom's house.

There may be some other thing happening between Mom and Dad that makes it uncomfortable for him to be around her . . . and therefore makes it uncomfortable for him to come and see you. I don't know which of them wanted the divorce, but Mom may be putting pressure on Dad to reunite with her, or Dad may be the one who wants a reunion, while Mom says no.

Of course, it may not be anything to do with reconciliation at all. Mom may be pressuring Dad for more money, or hassling him about something else, which causes him to avoid coming near the house.

Or perhaps, if you're a girl, you look so much like your mom did when she was younger that it's painful for Dad. He looks at you and is reminded of Mom, and that's just too painful for him to deal with.

And then, of course, it's possible that your dad hasn't got as good a reason as one of those. If your parents have been divorced for a while, your dad might have met someone new. Maybe he's seeing so much of her that he has little time for anything else — including, unfortunately, you. There could be some other not-so-good reason, too. It could be that money's tight and he's embarrassed to tell you, "I can't take you to the movies or out for dinner or anything. We'll have to stay home, eat hot dogs, and not do anything special this weekend." He might find it easier not to see you than to tell you that. (Of course he's wrong, but as you very well know, parents mess up too.)

If you do think the problem might be something you've said or done, call your dad (or, better yet, ask to see him in person if that's possible) and tell him you're wondering if your doing such-and-such may be the reason he doesn't want to see you as often. Tell him you're sorry, and offer to stop doing (fill in the blank), if that will make it possible to see him more often. (And then hold to what you said and watch your behavior!)

If you don't think it's anything you've done, sit down with him in person (if possible), or over the phone, and tell him that you really miss seeing him regularly. Emphasize that you love and need your dad, and that you'd like to see him more often. Ask him to be open and honest with you about what the problem really is, so that you can work it out. If he doesn't like coming to the house to pick you up, maybe you could bike or take a bus over to his house, or maybe he'd pay for a taxi. If it's something else, if he'll just tell you what the problem is, you can put your heads together and figure out a solution.

And, if your parents happen to have a friendly divorce and can communicate decently, enlist your mom's help. If she and your dad still talk nicely to each other, maybe she can help him realize that he's hurting you, that you love and need him, and that you want to see him more often. Besides, maybe he'll be more honest with her about the real nature of the problem.

Of course, there are lots of things that keep family and friends apart. It could be that your dad is launching a new business, or has been overloaded by his employer, really is overwhelmingly busy, and is sincerely pressed for time. If that's the case, it's probably a temporary situation and will resolve itself shortly. All you need to do is to be patient, and things may soon right themselves without any effort on your part.

But it never hurts to speak up and tell him! At least, your dad needs to know — and will want to know — that it matters to you.

Finally, since you asked about your dad, I've answered that way. My answer would be the same if it were your mom who wasn't seeing you often enough.

Q: *Are my parents going to start dating other people?*

A: Very likely. And it will probably feel weird to you, at least at first, to see your mom going out on dates, or to see your dad invite some woman over to have dinner with him. But remember, your parents aren't married anymore, so they aren't being disloyal. There's no reason they shouldn't date other people.

Do you or your friends go out on dates? Many of the same reasons that you and your friends date apply to your mom and dad too. Just as you enjoy the company of people of the opposite sex, so do they. Just as you enjoy a bit of romance and excitement, the companionship, and even the pleasure of chasing or being chased, so do they. Just as you enjoy going to concerts and other events with someone of the opposite sex, so do they. And just as you like to share your life with someone you like a lot, and hope to eventually find one person to settle down with, so do they.

Q: *If my mom gets married again, will I have to call her new husband "Dad"?*

A: Definitely not — unless you want to. The names that kids call their stepparents are many and varied. You can call your new stepdad — when and if you have one — by some variant of the "Dad" label such as "Pop." An old-fashioned approach to the situation was for the child to call the stepdad by "Uncle" plus his first name. That isn't done much anymore, but it could be an answer for you. You can call

him by just his first name — "Allen" or "Clay" or "George,"
or whatever it is — if he agrees to that. Or you can think up
a cute nickname to call him by. You might even like him well
enough that you *want* to call him "Dad." Or "Dad Allen,"
to differentiate him from your birth father. But you certainly
don't *have* to call him "Dad." You *have* a dad. And your
new stepfather will respect that.

Q: *If I don't like Mom's new husband, can I move in with
Dad?*

A: That's a matter to be settled among you, your mom, and
your dad. If your mom and your dad agree to it, there's no
reason not to. But give her new husband a chance. Be sure
you really don't like him. Be sure you're not just holding it
against him that he's trying to take Dad's place or that he's
simply not Dad.

After you really know him and perhaps have lived under
the same roof with him for a while, if you still feel the same
way, talk to your mom and dad about the possibility of
moving in with Dad. Mom may or may not be agreeable;
Dad may or may not agree too. (If he works long hours, for
example, he may feel it's best for you to stay with Mom.)
But if Mom and Dad agree, it's certainly do-able.

Approach Mom gently. After all, she loves her new
husband, and you won't win points with Mom by telling
her you don't like the man or by calling him names! But if
you can point to specific things her new husband does (or
doesn't do) that are a problem for you, she may understand
better. She may agree to let you move . . . or she may help
you and her new husband get along better. (Maybe there
are changes you both can make that would help you to feel

better about him and not so eager to leave. Learning to work out problems in relationships is a very important skill you'll need all your life!)

Q: *I love Mom and I miss Mom, but it's kind of nice around the house since she moved out. The other day she asked me how I'm handling her being gone. That's when I realized it's not totally awful having her gone. What do I say to her the next time she asks?*

A: You can be honest, but phrase your answer diplomatically. I'm assuming the reason it's "not totally awful having her gone" and "it's kind of nice around the house" is that there was arguing, or some other form of conflict, when she lived there.

You can certainly say to Mom, "Gee, I really miss having you around, but I have to admit it's nice to not have all that fighting going on anymore. I hated hearing you and Dad argue all the time." Or, "Well, to tell you the truth, as much as I miss seeing you all the time, the peacefulness is nice. There were always those times when you and Dad weren't talking, and it was rough on me. Now things are much more relaxed, and it's an easier atmosphere, even though I sure miss having you around."

If it's true, you might try this: "Since you left, I've felt more grown up. You sometimes forget that I'm not a little kid any more."

Whatever your reasons for "not totally awful," try to let her know — in a loving way — that you love *her* but not always the way she *behaves*. And isn't that exactly the way she feels about you? She'll understand.

Q: *Since Dad moved out, Mom talks to me differently —
almost like I were a friend of hers instead of her child.
Sometimes she tells me stuff I'm not comfortable hearing.
How do I stop her?*

A: You need to tell your mom that you're not comfortable
with some of the things she tells you. There are plenty of
parents who make the mistake of trying to turn their kids
into companions and friends in the wake of a divorce. But
that isn't the proper role for a child (of any age other than
adult). Wait till Mom tells you something that specifically
makes you uncomfortable. Then tell her that you don't feel
comfortable listening to that kind of thing, because she's still
your mom, and as much as you love her, you're her
daughter (or son), not her adult friend.

Whenever she tells you something you're not comfortable
hearing, tell her she's crossed the boundary again. (An
expression some people use is "T.M.I.," which stands for
"Too Much Information." Saying "T.M.I." may be useful in
this case.) After a while she'll get the message and learn
which things you're comfortable hearing and which you're
not. Parents are human too and make mistakes just as kids
do — just as everyone does.

Q: *My folks got divorced, and I moved in with my dad. I see
my mom two weekends a month. She's always taking me
shopping when I see her, and she buys me all kinds of cool
stuff.*

*I know — that sounds like heaven, not like a problem,
right? But here's the thing: I know she's short of money. I
hear her complaining to Dad, and I hear her on the phone
with Grandma. I don't think she can afford to buy me all*

those clothes and videogames and CDs and stuff. And I feel guilty when she gives them to me.

I promise you I'm not asking her for stuff. I've even told her I don't need anything else. But she keeps buying me all this stuff anyhow! It's getting so sometimes I even think about just not going to see her. What can I do?

A: An old friend of mine had an expression for fathers who had moved out of the house and weren't around their kids all the time. They tried to "buy their love" by spending money extravagantly on them when they saw them. He called these fathers, "Uncle Daddy, the ice-cream man." I'm told that in California they're called "Disneyland Dads." And your mother is the female version: "Mall Mom."

Sometimes this kind of behavior is caused by guilt. The parent isn't around to be a full-time mom or dad anymore, so he or she tries to make it up to the child (or teen) by spending money. It might be a matter of buying a pair of the most expensive sports shoes, frequent visits to a favorite theme park, shopping trips for stuff the kid doesn't need, or a "whirlwind" weekend with a ballgame, ice show, the movies, and dinner out in a nice restaurant, too. Some parents try to win their kids' love through spending money on them.

Sometimes this kind of behavior is caused not by guilt but by competition. One of the parents is competing with the other for their child's love. Mom may, in an effort to get her son or daughter to love her more than the kid loves his or her father, buy all kinds of presents, or stock the house with the kid's favorite foods (even if they're not healthy), or take the kid to lots of great places. . . . You get the idea. Anything to make the kid think, *Isn't my mom cool?! Look at all the stuff she bought me!*

Except that it doesn't always work. You're the proof of that. You're old enough to understand that your mom can't afford all the goodies she's buying you, and instead of her winning you over, she's driving you away.

More often it's the parent you live with only part-time who plays the part of Mall Mom or Disneyland Daddy. He or she is the happy, fun, generous parent who gives the kid lots of presents on visiting weekends. The rest of the time, the custodial parent has to discipline the kid, make sure homework and chores are done, rules are followed . . . and he or she doesn't have a chance to look good against the parent who's handing out all the goodies.

There are always exceptions to "sometimes," of course. There are plenty of custodial parents who, either because of guilt or competition, try to buy their kids' love in the same ways I've described above.

So to come back to your question of what you should do, here's what I suggest: Sit down with your mom and have a talk with her. Tell her, "Look, I love you, and I know you love me. You don't have to buy me all that stuff. I don't want you to buy me all that stuff. I'm not comfortable with it. Please stop." You might even add, "Lately, sometimes I feel like not coming over to visit you. I keep thinking that if I stay at Dad's, you won't be able to spend all that money on me. Do you know what I mean? It doesn't make me feel good. It makes me feel bad. Please stop."

Q: *Dad just doesn't understand! He goes and moves out of the house and then expects me to treat him like I always did! It's not fair! He moved out, left Mom and me, and then if I snap at him just a little, he gets this cold tone in his voice and* *says, "Simmer down!" He expects me to love him like I always did, but how can I after what he did?!*

A: Anger at the parent who moved out is understandable. But if you've been carrying this hurt and anger around inside you more than a couple of months, I'd suggest professional counseling. I'm not talking about long-term therapy; a few sessions with a counselor may well do it.

Do you know the circumstances behind the divorce? Do you *know* that Dad left of his own accord and not because Mom asked him to? Of course you're hurt, and it's understandable that you would be angry for a while, but please remember that your dad did not do this *to you.* He left *your mom* — whether it was his own choice or hers.

Sometimes innocent people get hurt in this world. You've probably heard the war term "collateral damage" — when innocent civilians get injured or killed during fighting. Divorces have a kind of "collateral damage" too — when kids get hurt in the process of the parents getting divorced.

I'm sure your dad didn't mean to hurt you and didn't want to leave you. But snapping at him doesn't help matters.

In a sense he's right. Though your anger is understandable, you do need to "simmer down" — not just in these individual incidents but in your overall anger. Please tell someone you'd like to talk to a professional soon.

Q: *Why don't people get off my mother's case?! My folks broke up, and they agreed that my brother and I should live with my dad. The three of us stayed in the house, and Mom moved to an apartment nearby.*

We see her often, and although I miss the old days, and I wish we were all still living together, I'm really okay with the way things are. Stuff happens. The world changes. But life goes on. You know?

What I am most definitely not okay with, though, is the way people talk. "Your mother left you?" "What's wrong with your mother?" "Is your mother sick?" "Is your mother on drugs?" "Doesn't your mother love you?" And other garbage.

What do I say to people who say these things? I can tell my friends to mind their own business, but I can't say that to grownups!

Why are they getting so upset anyhow?

A: In the "old days" — not that long ago — it was rare for a mother to leave her kids, rare for a father to have custody, and also not that common for a woman to work outside the house once she had kids. Now everything's changed.

Fathers (I'm not talking only about divorced dads now) are more involved with their kids — a good thing, for sure. Mothers are able to work outside the home without everyone thinking it's terrible. Another good thing. And sometimes fathers get custody of their kids after a divorce, which can also be good.

If your situation is good for you, good for your mom, and good for your dad, then that's a good thing too! And you're right . . . it isn't any of the neighbors' business. (But you know how people talk and gossip!)

Why are they getting upset? Because people love to find fault with others — sad fact, but true — and because many people still think a mother should always take care of her kids.

What can you do about it? With your friends, you can say, "Hey, I'm okay with the way things are. And by the way, I love my mom, so get off her case!" With older people you can say, "This arrangement works for our family. Mom hasn't deserted us. She's still very much a part of our lives. And there's nothing wrong with her, or with the way our family is now. Now, I'd really rather not talk about it anymore."

Q: *My mom left our family. Not just my dad but our whole family. She made it plain she didn't want to be a mom anymore. She doesn't see us, doesn't call often, and it isn't just a case of divorce. She left all of us. Why? We kids (I'm the oldest of three) got into the usual amount of trouble, but none of us is really a bad kid. Honest!*

I don't know what we did wrong, and I don't know how to get Mom to come back. (Even though I'm hurt that she left us, I still love her.)

A: And I'm sure your mom still loves you too, but . . . although she still loves you, she may be one of those people who never should have become a parent.

Not everyone is cut out to be a parent. Parenting is hard work. Parenting requires patience. Parenting isn't something everyone in the world is good at automatically — or enjoys. Some people just can't handle it.

Frankly, as rough as it is for you to have an absent parent, it's probably less harmful and less hurtful than having an uncaring parent.

I know it doesn't make it hurt any less that she left you, but the truth is, you may actually be better off this way. The most important thing for you to know is that it's not because of anything you did. It's not because you and the other kids in the family were too bad or too difficult. The problem is with your mom. And it's probably not anything that can be "fixed."

Maybe — although there are no promises! — when she's had a some time to be away from the demands of being a parent, she'll miss you and start visiting more often. (But maybe not.) Meanwhile remember these three things:

1. She still loves you — she just can't handle parenting.

2. It's not because of anything you — or any of the kids in your family — did.

3. You're fortunate that you still have your dad to love you and take care of you.

Q: *My folks got divorced, and in the beginning my dad came around to see us regularly, but little by little he stopped seeing us. And he lives right here in town! At first I would call him and ask him when he was going to see us again, but he was always "too busy" or he "didn't know" — or else I would get his machine and leave a message, and he wouldn't even bother to call me back. My mother says he still loves us, but it's obvious he doesn't. (He didn't even spend a lot of time with us when he and my mom were married.)*

My sister keeps bugging my mother to hurry up and get married again so we'll have a father. But I don't think that's the answer.

Any advice?

A: Wow, that's a toughie. Okay, from the top, a few points:

• If your father didn't spend much time with you even during the marriage, he might be one of those people who just isn't cut out for parenting. That doesn't mean he doesn't love you. It does mean he doesn't know how to be a good, involved father.

• On the other hand, that might not be it at all. It might be a situation in which seeing you reminds him of his failed marriage, and he isn't dealing with it well. You might try keeping yourself in his thoughts by sending things to him — funny greeting cards by mail, letters and jokes via email. Perhaps once he gets past the hurt he feels, he'll be better able to deal with seeing you. And by sending stuff to him, you're keeping the lines of communication open. He won't wonder whether you'd even welcome him when he's ready to see you.

• Your sister isn't altogether wrong. Of course getting a new stepdad wouldn't replace your father or take away the hurt of having him ignore you. But having a loving father figure in the house would be a good thing on a number of levels. For one thing, you'll feel better about yourself when you see that an older man, a father figure, really loves you and enjoys spending time with you. For another thing, it's good to have a dad you can go to with questions and problems that you'd like to discuss with a male parent. So, if and when your mom remarries, you'll benefit from it.

• In the meantime, while there's no male parent in the house, it might help you to find some other person who could be a kind of "substitute father" to you. This might be a grandfather or uncle. Or it might be the husband of one of your mother's friends, or the father of one of your friends. It might be someone you know from the neighborhood. When I was eighteen, and I moved to my own apartment, I made friends with the pharmacist in the neighborhood drugstore and made him into a father-substitute. (My own dad was dead.) Choose wisely. Don't just latch onto the first older man who seems vaguely fatherly. And don't expect him to totally replace your father. But having a father figure you can talk to and get good advice from is a good thing when your own father isn't making himself available.

• Above all, remember, if your father doesn't come to see you, *it's not because of you or anything you did.* It's obviously *his* problem. (The fact that he's not seeing you or your sister either only proves what I'm saying. Surely you both didn't do something that upset him or made him angry.) Whether he doesn't have good fatherly feelings or can't deal with being reminded that his marriage failed, or whatever the problem is, it's *his* problem. It's not you!

Q: *How long can a separation last? My parents split up last year (over a year ago), but they're still not officially divorced. You know that expression, "Waiting for the other shoe to drop"? That's how I feel.*

As long as they're only "separated" and not divorced, I keep hoping they'll get back together. Well, so far they haven't gotten divorced . . . but they haven't gotten back together either. They just stay separated! How long can two parents remain "separated" without having to make up their minds?

A: Unfortunately for you, there's no law requiring them to "make up their minds."

As you may recall from a question early in this chapter, there are two kinds of separations. One is a trial separation, in which a couple tries living separately to see if they think they're better off that way rather than married and living together. The other isn't a trial — the couple knows they want to break up; they just haven't finalized the divorce yet.

I have no way of knowing which type of separation your parents are in the middle of. But if over a year has passed and they haven't gotten back together, it doesn't look very hopeful that they're going to.

Sometimes couples who separate and intend it to be permanent don't rush to get a divorce. There are various reasons for that; those reasons don't matter very much here. Most of them have nothing to do with any thoughts of getting back together. To give you just one example: A divorce costs money. (Lawyers don't work cheaply!) If neither partner is in a hurry to remarry, it may be enough for them just to separate. Now that they're not living together, they're happier, and getting fully divorced is less important to them.

Of course, I can understand that a separation, without a divorce, could send a mixed message. You don't know which way things are going to go. But, once again, if they've been apart for over a year, chances don't look good for their getting back together. You'd be safest treating the separation as if it were a divorce. Your parents are no longer married, no matter what label they're putting on the breakup.

Q: *My dad has a temper. When he lived with us, he yelled a lot and sometimes threw things. Now that my parents are divorced, it doesn't happen so much, but there are still times when I'm at Dad's house and he blows up. And one day he came to the house and got mad at Mom. I thought he was going to hit her. He tried, but she ran to the neighbors'.*

I'm embarrassed to tell anyone. What should I do?

A: First of all, please get over being embarrassed. You are not responsible for your father's actions. (Or your mother's, or anyone's but your own.) No one is going to think any less of you for what your father does.

You need to make sure you are safe. (Maybe you could help make sure your mother is safe too.) You need to talk to someone — someone besides your mother. Here are some possibilities: the police, your school guidance counselor or psychologist, your doctor, the youth director or clergy at your religious congregation, a trusted teacher or coach, a grandparent.

Your father may be ordered by the court to take anger management classes, or to get psychological counseling. If his problem stems from abusing alcohol or other substances, he may be ordered to do something about that. Won't it be nice when you don't have to be afraid of him anymore? Meanwhile, until he gets a grip on his temper, you don't need to go and see him at his house or let him come to yours. You can insist on meeting him only in a public place. He is less likely to get violent in a restaurant or movie theater or park.

If he's really a danger to your family, your mom can get a restraining order from the police that will stop your dad from coming to your house. This will help protect her from him, too.

Nobody has the right to harm you or your mother. There are laws to protect you. Don't be afraid to get the help you need. And keep in mind that your dad needs help too — help in controlling his temper. The same people — police and judges — who can help you and your mom stay safe can also help see that your dad gets the help he needs.

Q: *When I come home from visiting my dad, my mom always asks me if I had a nice time. Most of the time I say yes, because most of the time I do have a nice time. Sometimes, though, when I say no, it seems to me that she's happy about it. Should I not tell her when I've had a good time? Should I make sure to tell her the things that went wrong? I think that might make her happier.*

I was talking about this with a friend of mine whose parents are divorced too. Brian's dad works long hours and never spent much time with him even before the divorce. So Brian's not used to seeing a lot of his father. When Brian goes to see his dad, his dad always asks, "Did you miss me?" Brian says he answers yes even though the truth is that he didn't. Brian probably spends more time with his dad now, since the divorce, than he did before. So he doesn't really miss him between visits.

But Brian wants to make his dad happy, just like I like making my mom feel good. So we tell them what we think they want to hear. Are we right?

A: Just keep telling your mom the truth, whatever it is. As I've said elsewhere in this book, parents are human. So, while it's wrong, your mom might be happy to think you enjoy yourself better at her house than at your dad's. But if you had a good time at your dad's, don't be afraid to say so. And don't look for little problems to report, just to make your mom happy.

As for your friend Brian, he can answer his father in a way that isn't dishonest but won't hurt his dad's feelings. When Brian's dad asks if he missed him, Brian can answer, "I'm always happy to see you!" or even be more honest than that and tell him, "Well, you know, I actually see more of you now than I did before!"

Kids shouldn't pretend to feel emotions they don't really feel, just to please their parents.

Q: *I tried to talk to my dad about my feelings about the divorce, but he told me, "It's not that big a deal. People get divorced all the time. Don't make mountains out of molehills." I can't understand. Are my feelings that unimportant to him? And doesn't it mean anything to him that he's not married to Mom anymore?*

A: Your dad is protecting himself. Unfortunately he's hurting you in the process. People sometimes make light of serious situations because they don't want to acknowledge how serious they really are. He's probably hurting inside, and the way he's coping is by pretending it really isn't important. But while he's trying to help himself, he's not helping you at all.

Please understand that your dad is not as unconcerned as he seems. He has "put on a mask" of not caring in order to hide and protect his own feelings.

But this doesn't help you at all. I have three suggestions for you:

1. Can you talk to your mom instead? Whether you're now living with your mom or your dad, and whether you're a boy or a girl, you can probably talk to your mom about your concerns and questions. This kind of conversation is always better in person. But maybe you live with your dad and you have a need to talk *right now,* and your dad isn't making himself open to this conversation with you. In that case, a phone call to your mom is better than just keeping your questions and feelings stuffed inside you.

2. If this is a conversation about divorce in general, or about your feelings, and your dad just won't talk and your mom isn't around for the moment, you can try talking to someone else. Throughout this book I've suggested people you might be able to talk to, from friends to relatives to teachers to youth leaders to school counselors to clergy to psychologists or other professionals.

3. If this is a talk you specifically need to have with your dad (for example, if it has to do with questions about your parents' divorce, rather than about divorce in general, or your feelings), you can try to make him understand how important this is to you. You can say (in whatever words are comfortable for you), "Hey, Dad, maybe it's no big deal to you, but it is to me. And it is to most kids whose parents get divorced. So please respect my feelings. You don't have to tell me anything that's too personal or private, but I really need to talk this out with you. Can we talk . . . please?"

Of course, if your questions wander into areas that are private between your dad and your mom — like why the marriage broke up in the first place — you need to respect your dad's privacy — and your mom's. Be sure you're not pushing your dad to talk about matters that intrude on your parents' privacy. Your dad may not want to say, "None of your business," but in fact some aspects of divorce *aren't* your business.

Q: *My mom wouldn't tell me why she and Dad broke up. But I overheard a conversation, and now I know it's because Dad was cheating on her. Now I don't feel the same way about Dad that I did before. How could he do that to her? I don't even like going over to his house anymore. But I don't know what to tell him when he asks why I don't want to see him.*

A: Unfaithfulness is certainly one of the reasons couples break up. And it's one of the things I have in mind when I say that the reason for a divorce may not really be something you need to know, but might be something private between your parents.

Here are some things for you to think about:

• You don't know for an absolute fact that it's true. You know only that your mother believes it.

• Assuming it's true, you don't know *why* he was unfaithful. While cheating is certainly a bad thing, there might be other facts that you're not aware of, things that might make what your dad did seem a little more understandable if you knew the whole story.

• In any case, what he did he did *to your mother.* I understand that you may feel protective of your mom: "How could he do that to her?!" But please remember that it doesn't really change anything between you and your dad. *You've* done things you shouldn't have, too, I'm sure.

Yes, your dad messed up. Big-time! But give him a break and remember that he's still your dad and he still loves you.

He messed up, and now he's paying for it. He lost his marriage and the chance to live with his kids. He's being punished. But it's not your place to add to that punishment. And it's not even your place to judge him when you don't know the whole story.

I'd suggest that the next time he asks why you don't want to see him, you tell him. Make it clear that Mom didn't *tell* you, that you found out by overhearing the information. But he deserves to know why his own child is turning away from him. Give him that much courtesy.

Q: *Before the divorce, I thought things seemed kind of tense around the house, and Dad was working late an awful lot of nights. I asked Mom, but she said everything was fine. I asked her several times, but she always insisted everything was okay. Then — boom — they announced they were getting a divorce. Now I feel like Mom was lying to me. It's not a good feeling. Is it possible everything really was all right, and the divorce was that sudden?*

A: Probably not, but your mom was more than likely either trying to protect you or lying to herself, rather than outright lying to you. She may have wanted to believe that everything was fine, so she told herself it was . . . and, of course, she would say the same thing to you, then. Or she may have realized there was a problem but *hoped* that things would straighten themselves out. So she told you everything was okay because she hoped that, in the end, things would work out, and she didn't want to worry you needlessly.

I'm not just "putting a spin" on her misinformation. In the one case, she is fooling herself but telling you what she thinks — or hopes — is true, even though it isn't. In the other case, she is being deliberately deceptive but doing it for a good reason — to protect you — while believing or at least hoping that everything *will* be all right in the end.

Of course, in the end, the divorce was more of a shock because you'd been led to believe that everything was okay, when it wasn't. This is unfortunate. But, on the other hand, suppose your parents were having trouble, and your mom told you, and then they worked it out and stayed together? You'd have been worrying and upset all for nothing. So don't be too rough on your mom. She meant the best for you.

Points to Remember

• Don't try to get your parents back together. You probably don't know the whole story. Trying to get them back together might feel good for you, but it probably won't work, and it really might not be a good thing altogether.

• Even if only one parent wanted the divorce, it's best not to get your hopes up about them getting back together.

• If your mom or dad is sad because of the divorce, you can think of some things that might make her or him feel better, but if not, don't feel bad. Remember, you're not responsible for their happiness.

• If a parent wanted a divorce but now is sad, it doesn't mean he or she would still like to be married.

• A "trial separation" means the couple is trying out living separately to see if it's better than being married to each other. The other kind of separation is when parents live apart before a divorce is final.

• If you're a teenager, there's a good chance the judge will give some consideration to your wishes as to which parent you want to live with, but he or she will not necessarily agree to what you want. There are many other factors to consider.

• If both your parents agree, you can see the parent you don't usually live with more often than just the days the judge set down in the divorce agreement.

- If you want to live with your other parent, think hard about your reasons. Make sure they're good ones. Then put the question to both your parents. And don't ask in a way that hurts anyone's feelings.

- If your non-custodial parent isn't seeing you regularly, are you sure you haven't been acting badly or hurting his or her feelings or pressuring him to "come home" when you visit? If the answer is no, it's probably got nothing to do with you. Talk to him or her about it.

- It's likely that eventually your parents will start dating other people.

- If your parents get remarried to new people, you don't have to call your mom's new husband "Dad" or your dad's new wife "Mom."

- If you don't like your parent's new husband or wife, it might be possible to move in with your other parent. But give the new husband or wife a chance, first. Make sure you're not just resenting him or her for "taking Dad's/Mom's place."

- If you miss having Dad around, but you enjoy the peace and quiet now that the fighting has stopped, you can say so honestly if he asks if you miss him. But phrase it tactfully. Don't hurt his feelings if you can help it.

- If your parent has started treating you as a friend since the divorce, and tells you things you're not comfortable hearing, you have the right to stop her or him. You can use a phrase like "T.M.I." [Too Much Information] to clue her that she's crossed a boundary.

• "Disneyland Dads" and "Mall Moms" try to "buy" their kids' love with presents or trips to amusement parks or other expensive stuff. This isn't a good thing. You can speak up and try to stop them.

• Don't be angry at the parent who moved out. He or she left your other parent — not you — and maybe not even by his or her own choice.

• If you stay angry for long, get professional help — short-term therapy to help you get over your anger.

• People are too often critical when a mom moves out and leaves the kids with the dad. But it's nobody's business but your family's, and you don't have to listen to their criticisms. You can tell them nicely that you don't want to hear it.

• Some people aren't cut out to be parents. A small number of moms and dads who get divorced stop seeing their kids because they are people who really never should have become parents in the first place. It doesn't mean your parent doesn't love you, and *it's not because of anything you did.*

• Sometimes parents get separated without going on to get divorced. This does not necessarily mean they are thinking of getting back together. They may just not feel any need to get divorced now or may not have the money it costs. The important thing, for them, was to stop living together, and so a separation serves their purpose. It's best if you think of them as "as good as divorced." Don't hold out hope that they'll reunite. It probably won't happen.

• If one of your parents gets unreasonably angry and abusive — hitting, throwing things, yelling in a threatening way — you need to tell someone. This is true whether his or her anger is directed at you or your other parent. Don't be embarrassed. You are not responsible for your parents' behavior. Get help!

• Don't pretend to feel emotions you don't really feel, just to please your parents.

• Even if you find out that one of your parents did something mean or bad to the other one to cause the divorce, *it's still between them*. If your mom cheated on your dad, or your dad did something cruel to your mom, that's still between them. Try not to let what he or she did affect the way you feel toward him or her. It's not between your parent and you.

10

A Few Last Words

Yes, it's tough enough being a teenager without your parents getting divorced. But, on the other hand, maybe your parents have been at each other's throat verbally, which hasn't been fun for you, either. And now maybe you're in for some much-needed peace and quiet. Or maybe your parents have been dumping on you, getting unduly angry over little things because they were upset with each other. And now maybe that's going to stop too — if not immediately, then in the not-too-distant future.

So you see, this cloud *can* have a silver lining.

I hope this book will be a good guide — and friend — to you as you work your way through the maze of dealing with divorced parents. (And, trust me, it *does* get easier.) Don't hesitate to lean on others too — on your friends (especially the ones who've been through this themselves), on the professionals I mentioned earlier in the book (like school counselors or clergy), on caring neighbors or parents of your friends — whoever can help you. There's no need to be embarrassed. Parents get divorced all the time, unfortunately, and it's nothing for you to feel uncomfortable or awkward about. Remember, *it's not about you.*

Here's to happier days ahead!

Index

adultery, 19, 123
advice
    getting from others, 30
    people to go to for, 91
affairs, 19, 123
alcohol, 89
anger
    getting out of your system, 34
    at parent who moves out, 112, 128
    parents at one another, 11, 15
    when dangerous, 119–120
arguing parents, 15–16, 95–96
blame for divorce, 5–6, 21
books
    finding comfort in, 32
    talking to parent about, 53
boyfriends, talking to, 31
California, children's custody
        preferences, 49
changes in life from divorce, 41–45
children
    deciding which parent to live with,
        99–100
    getting parents back together,
        96–97
    wishes taken into consideration in
        custody, 49
'collateral damage' from divorces, 112
college plans, talking to parent about,
        53
comfort
    finding during and after divorce,
        40
    finding in troubled times, 29–33
    in parent's new home, 55–59
counseling, 2
crying when sad, 35–36
custody
    arrangements, 47–51
    scheduling visits, 100
    visiting a parent who lives at a
        distance, 71–75
"Dad," 106–107
dating of divorced parents, 101, 104,
        106
decisions, making during your parents'
        divorce, 87–93
depression
    helping parents with, 12, 97, 98
    seeking help for, 13
    in your family, 10

divorce, 13
    blame for, 5, 21
    custody arrangements, 47–51
    dealing with changes caused by,
        41–45
    not fault of children, 31
    vs. separation, 98–99
Divorce Helpbook for Kids, The, 1–2
domestic violence, 119, 129
drugs, 88, 100
email, 73
embarrassment over parents' divorce,
        119
emotions
    See also feelings
    romantic relationships, starting, 31
exercise
    finding comfort in, 35
    for releasing anger, 40
father figures, 116–117
feelings
    See also emotions
    not hurting a parent's, 121
    writing about in journal, 3–4
fighting
    of parents, 15–17, 95–96
    when to get help, 119–120
financial problems, 23, 25, 41, 109–110
friends
    divorced parents who make their
        children into, 109, 127
    talking to about your parents'
        divorce, 3–4, 30–31, 91
girlfriends, talking to, 31
guilt over parents' divorce, 5–6, 21
help, seeking, 13, 131–132
home, finding comfort in, 32
Instant Messaging (IM), 73
interviews for distant parent
        (videotape), 74–75
joint custody, 47
journals, keeping, 3
love
    finding comfort in, despite divorce,
        33–34
    parents' for their children, 18
lying, of parents, 124–125
mailing letters to parents, 73
marriage too young, 19
messages, asking kids to carry, 1, 77–80
"Mom," 106–107

money troubles, 23, 25, 41, 53,
        109–110
moving
        after your parents' divorce, 41–45
        finding comfort in, 33
        keeping in touch with absent
                parent, 71–75
music, 32, 53
Parent Trap, The (movie), 95
parents
        deciding which to live with, 48–51,
                99–100, 107, 127
        competing over children, 110–111
        dating after divorce, 104, 106
        disrespecting each other, 24
        getting back together, 96–97, 126
        jobs, taking more, 41
        keeping in touch with, 73
        living with one, 48–51, 127
        lying, 124–125
        married too young, 19
        new home, feeling comfortable in,
                55–59
        sadness of, 98, 126
        unfair tactics of, 77–85
        unfaithfulness of, 123
        unhappiness, and divorce, 6
        who live in different cities, 71–75
personal 800 numbers, 74
pets as comfort, 30
phoning parents, 73, 105
primary custody, 47
problems
        divorce doesn't solve life's, 8, 13
        money troubles, 23, 25
relationships
        parents dating after divorce, 104,
                106
        with boyfriends and girlfriends, 31
remarriage, 116, 127
resources for children of divorced
                parents, 2–3
room of your own, 57
sadness
        and crying, 35
        of parents after divorce, 98, 126
safety, making sure you are, 119
school, parent going to, 49
security, obtaining in troubled times,
                29–33
separations, 98–99, 117–118, 126
sex, 88

smoking, 89
sports, taking comfort in, 35
spying, parent asking child to, 80–85
stepparents
        benefits of, 116
        getting along with, 127
        name of, 106
studying, finding comfort in, 32
substance abuse, 88, 100
surprise of divorce, 15, 25
talking
        about your problems, 2–4
        to parent during visits, 52–55,
                61–68
        to parents about unfair treatment,
                9
        to people for advice, 30–31, 91
        respecting privacy, 122–123
teenagers, using this book, 1–2
telephoning parents, 73, 105
therapy, 2
        finding comfort in troubled times,
                29–33
        journal-writing, 3–4
T.M.I. ("Too Much Information"), 109,
                127
topics to talk with parents about,
                53–55
trial separation, 98–99, 117–118, 126
unfair tactics
        asking kids to spy, 80–85
        carrying messages between parents,
                77–80
        when a parent moves, 44
unfair treatment, talking to parents
                about, 9
unfaithfulness of a parent, 19, 123
unhappiness. *See* sadness
videotapes, making for a parent,
                74–75
violence, 119, 129
visiting a parent, 51–60, 61–68
        changes after divorce, 41–45
        at a distance, 71–75
        schedule for, 100
weekend custody, 48
withdrawal as reaction to troubles, 11
writing in journal, 3